CIVIL RIGHTS
STRUGGLES
around the
WORLD

OPEN THE JAIL DOORS— WE WANT TO *ENTER*

THE DEFIANCE CAMPAIGN AGAINST APARTHEID LAWS

South Africa, 1952

STUART A. **KALLEN**

T F C B

TWENTY-FIRST CENTURY BOOKS ■ **MINNEAPOLIS**

To Teddy Belle for her laughter, love, song, and support

Twenty-First Century Books
A division of Lerner Publishing Group, Inc.
241 First Avenue North
Minneapolis, MN 55401 U.S.A.

Website address: www.lernerbooks.com

Library of Congress Cataloging-in-Publication Data

Kallen, Stuart A., 1955–
    Open the jail doors—we want to enter: the defiance camplaign against apartheid laws, South Africa,
1952/ by Stuart A. Kallen.
        p.   cm. — (Civil rights struggles around the world)
    Includes bibliographical references and index.
    ISBN 978-0-8225-8969-3 (lib. bdg. : alk. paper)
    1. Anti-apartheid movements—South Africa. 2. Apartheid—South Africa. 3. South Africa—Politics and
government—1978–1989. 4. African National Congress. I. Title.
DT1757.K356 2011
323.168—dc22   2009042436

Manufactured in the United States of America
1 – CG – 7/15/10

CONTENTS

DEFIANCE AGAINST UNJUST LAWS

In the early hours of June 26, 1952, dawn broke over the city of Port Elizabeth, South Africa. Because of the city's location, far south of the equator, it was a cold midwinter day. But the chilly winds and gray skies could not stop twenty-five men and five women from carrying out their simple plan of action. They walked into the New Brighton railway station and sat down in the waiting room. If the men and women had been Afrikaners, or white people of European descent, they would have gone unnoticed. But the people in the waiting room were black South Africans who passed under a sign that read "Europeans Only." The group was taking part in the Campaign of Defiance against Unjust Laws instituted by the African National Congress (ANC). The campaign was organized to defy a series of laws known as apartheid. The word *apartheid*, Afrikaans for "apartness, or separateness," describes a system of racial segregation put in place in 1948 by South Africa's governing National Party.

The protesters, or defiers, wore ANC armbands and chanted, "Mayibuye Africa!" or "Africa come back to me!" Almost immediately after the defiers took their seats, a white police sergeant approached the group's thirty-two-year-old leader, Raymond Mhlaba. The officer informed him that he was breaking the law. Mhlaba replied that his group was deliberately carrying out a political act and asked the officer to arrest them. Other police officers were called, and the defiers were handcuffed and led from the station. Mhlaba later recalled with a smile that as they were taken into custody, police had to march the group over a passenger bridge marked "Europeans Only."

Hours after the Port Elizabeth defiers were detained, fifty-three protesters were arrested in Boksburg, near Johannesburg, South Africa's largest city. This group of forty-three blacks and ten people of

Indian ancestry entered an area that was restricted by pass laws. This meant that the only nonwhites who could walk into the district were required to carry government-issued passes. The Boksburg group was led by Nana Sita, a native of Gujarat, India. Under apartheid, the rights of Indians were also severely restricted. So were the rights of those people classified as "colored," or of mixed race.

RALLYING TO THE NATIONAL CALL

And so it went throughout the day. In Worcester nine mixed-race and African people were arrested for standing in the whites-only

A sign warns "Kaffirs," a derogatory name for southern African blacks, against entering a white neighborhood in South Africa in the late 1940s.

line in the post office. In Durban, Jewish lawyer and Communist Sam Kahn was jailed for attending a city council meeting. Kahn was defying an apartheid law called the Suppression of Communism Act, which restricted Communists from public gatherings.

The first night of the protests, the ANC held a meeting in Johannesburg that did not end until eleven o'clock. When the group dispersed, they were met by a row of armed police lining the street on both sides. The entire group was arrested. As they willingly piled into police wagons, they sang "Nkosi Sikelel' iAfrika," or "Lord Bless Africa," a protest song that would become the national anthem of South Africa in 1994. The ANC members were charged with violating curfew. The curfew law required Africans to carry special permits to walk within the city after eleven o'clock.

Some of those arrested on June 26 were well-known antiapartheid leaders. They included Walter Sisulu, secretary-general of the ANC; Nelson Mandela, lawyer and president of the ANC Youth League (YL); and Yusuf Cachalia, secretary-general of the South African Indian Congress. But most of the 250 resisters who were jailed the first day of the Defiance Campaign were average citizens. Some were sympathetic whites. In September 1953, Mandela described those who participated in the Campaign of Defiance of Unjust Laws: "Factory and office workers, doctors, lawyers, teachers, students, and the clergy; Africans, Coloureds, Indians, and Europeans, old and young. [They] all rallied to the national call and defied the pass laws and the curfew and the railway apartheid regulations."

SPREADING LIKE WILDFIRE

Normally, those who violated apartheid were not jailed but ordered to pay a relatively small fine. Participants in the Defiance Campaign demanded trials where they could voice their complaints against the government and its discriminatory rules. After bravely refusing to pay fines imposed by judges, the defiers were sent to jail from four to six weeks. But this didn't slow the movement. The mass imprisonment only encouraged others to join the Defiance Campaign. As Mandela said, "It spread throughout the country like wildfire." In July fifteen hundred men and women defied. In August more than two thousand went to jail. When Mandela was arrested again, under the Suppression of Communism Act, the courtroom was filled with supporters singing Defiance Campaign songs in beautiful lilting harmonies. The judge was forced to adjourn the court and hold the trial at a later date.

Those who participated in the Defiance Campaign followed the plan of the ANC. There was no violence and no resistance to arrest.

The goal was to fill the jails to overflowing and cause the police and judicial branches of government to break down. The ANC hoped the chaos of the civil disobedience would force government leaders to repeal the apartheid laws. It did not work out that way, however. As South Africa's white prime minister Dr. D. F. Malan stated at the time, "The Government will make full use of the machinery at its disposal to quell any disturbances, and, thereafter, deal adequately with those responsible." Following this pronouncement, government repression increased dramatically. Defiers were sentenced to hard labor for up to two years. Some under the age of twenty were whipped or severely beaten with canes.

By the end of 1952, most ANC leaders had been arrested, and the government continued to enforce apartheid for decades. Still, the Defiance Campaign attracted international attention to South Africa's unjust separation of the races. The New York Times reported that South Africa was headed toward a "shipwreck" and called apartheid a "false, immoral and repugnant" system. The Times of London wrote that South African racial policies were "flagrant violations of human rights [that involved] the arrest of 4,000 people engaged in passive resistance against segregation laws." Perhaps most important, American civil rights activists viewed the courageous Defiance Campaign as an inspiration. Before long, Martin Luther King Jr. and others would be defying segregation in Alabama and elsewhere in the United States using similar tactics.

The Defiance Campaign began a movement that would eventually triumph. But before it did, people were imprisoned and blood was shed by three generations of South Africans. Thousands died fighting for equal rights. They never saw the day when Nelson Mandela was elected South Africa's first black president. But when President Mandela stood on a podium in May 1994, before thousands of free South Africans, he understood that his election would not have been possible were it not for the Defiance Campaign. It was the first step on a long, hard journey to freedom that took forty-two years and countless sacrifices.

CHAPTER 1

THE CAPE
COLONY

Van Riebeeck implanted the [first seeds] of Black oppression as he ushered the Africanization of poverty, destruction of African families, erosion of African cultures . . . and all forms of oppressions in South Africa."

—J. C. Buthelezi, South African author, 2002

On July 26, 1952, during the Defiance Campaign, more than fifty protesters deliberately defied apartheid pass laws in Boksburg, South Africa. The protesters were immediately arrested. While being led to police vans, the defiers began to loudly sing, "Jan van Riebeeck has stolen our freedom." The protesters were not singing about a politician who had helped institute apartheid in 1948. They were referring to the man known as the founding father of South Africa.

To white South Africans of European descent, or Afrikaners, Commander Jan van Riebeeck was the George Washington of their nation. To the blacks, Indians, and mixed-race people of twentieth-century South Africa, van Riebeeck was to blame for more than three centuries of slavery and oppression. However, when Jan van Riebeeck landed his wooden sailing ship on the southwestern tip of Africa in April 1652, he had no intentions of founding a nation. Nor did he actively plan to enslave the indigenous (local) people who lived there.

Commander van Riebeeck, accompanied by his wife and son and a crew of eighty-two men and eight women, was carrying out orders for the Dutch United East India Company. This trading company, *Vereenigde Oost-Indische Compagnie,* or VOC, in Dutch, was established in 1602 in the Netherlands. It was the first multinational corporation. Traders bought spices in Indonesia, silk, cotton, and porcelain in China and textiles in India. While traveling the

Jan van Riebeeck settled on the southwestern tip of Africa for the Dutch United East India Company in 1652.

trade routes between eastern Asia and Europe, VOC ships sailed past the Cape of Good Hope at the southwestern tip of the African continent. At this point in the long, dangerous journey, ship provisions were running low. Van Riebeeck's mission was to set up a supply, or refreshment, station along Table Bay. Table Bay is located at the northern end of the Cape Peninsula, which stretches south to the Cape of Good Hope. The station was to provide water, vegetables, fruit, meat, and medical assistance to VOC sailors.

When van Riebeeck's crew landed on the site, it was already inhabited by two groups of people. The indigenous Khoikhoi, or Khoi, had been living as seminomads in southern Africa since at least the fifth century A.D. These people, referred to disparagingly as the Hottentots by the Dutch, hunted and gathered food in the area. The Khoi also

This modern image shows a Khoi child in front of a traditional home. The homes are made of woven reed mats carefully placed over branches that are curved and firmly positioned in the ground.

grazed large herds of cattle in the fields around Table Bay. Another indigenous group in the area, the San, were nomadic hunter-gathers. The Dutch called them Bushmen. The San often passed through the region in search of game, which their hunters skillfully pursued with bows and poison-tipped arrows.

Van Riebeeck's party was not the first group of Dutch settlers in the region. Previous explorers had coexisted peacefully with the local people. In the introduction to his journal, van Riebeeck described what he had learned about the people of southern Africa:

> [Some] will say that the natives are brutal and cannibals, from whom no good can be expected, and that we will have to be continually on our guard, but this is a vulgar error. . . . [By] treating the natives kindly and gratefully, paying for whatever is obtained [from] them, also filling some of the natives' stomachs with peas or beans, which they are very partial to, nothing need be feared.

FROM COMPANY TO COLONY

While the Khoi were not perceived as unfriendly, van Riebeeck soon discovered that survival was extremely difficult for the Europeans in southern Africa. The place they settled, called the Cape Flats, was a sandy area that stretched 20 miles (32 kilometers) along the Cape Peninsula. Access to the rest of Africa was cut off by the high, craggy peaks of the Hottentots-Holland mountain range to the east. This land was dry and infertile. The expedition could hardly feed itself there. By September of the first year, the daily diet for the employees of the VOC was limited to a small amount of peas and barley. Weakened from lack of food, at least forty crew members died from disease within the first six months. Instead of supplying food to sailors, van Riebeeck was forced to beg for rice and salted meat from company ships as they passed around the Cape of Good Hope.

Eventually, the Europeans were able to establish a small colony in southern Africa and build a fort there. When the fort was finished, the settlers began the long, difficult task of fertilizing the soil, planting seeds, and maintaining vegetable gardens and fruit orchards. In the years that followed, Dutch trade with the East prospered and the number of ships sailing past the Cape Colony increased. The settlers had to plant even bigger gardens and graze more cattle to supply the sailors. This increased tensions with the Khoi and San, who objected to losing large amounts of their land. But these people had no written language or legal systems. They had no deeds to show ownership of the land. For van Riebeeck, this was an excuse to refuse the locals' property claims.

By 1657 the rapidly expanding VOC fleet required more provisions than van Riebeeck's crew could supply. To help satisfy the company needs, a group of Dutch settlers, called free burghers, was sent from the Netherlands to the settlement known as Cape Town. Unlike others at the small colony, the new arrivals were not VOC employees. They were

THE CLICKING **KHOI LANGUAGE**

When Dutch settlers first arrived in southern Africa, they were greeted by nomadic herders. The indigenous Africans called themselves the Khoikhoi, which means "people people," or "real people," in the Khoekhoe language. The Europeans referred to them as "Hottentots," the Dutch word for someone who stutters. In modern times, this term is considered a racial insult. It came about because of a specific characteristic of the Khoekhoe language. About three-quarters of the words in Khoekhoe begin with a click. There are four types of clicks, made by the tongue on the roof of the mouth. One has been described as sounding like a cork being drawn from a bottle, and another sounds like the gurgling of water pouring out of a bottle. The third click is similar to the sound Europeans make when urging a horse to trot, and the last type of click is said to be indescribable.

encouraged to grow crops that could be sold to the VOC. But they were not allowed to produce anything already grown by company employees.

While the new settlers tended fields, VOC directors expected Khoi workers to do the difficult manual labor, such as building houses, wharves, warehouses, and roads. However, the majority of locals did not wish to give up their traditional lives to work for the low wages offered by the Dutch. The Khoi also refused to trade with the Europeans because the VOC only offered low-quality goods in trade for the meat and milk produced by the natives.

Because the Khoi did not want to work with the VOC, the company had to rethink its goals. Initially, it only intended to maintain a small, self-sustaining refreshment station. But it was forced to encourage European immigration to Cape Town so it could colonize a larger territory.

SLAVES AND BOERS

In its first step toward colonization, the VOC began bringing in slaves from East Africa, Madagascar, Mozambique, India, Ceylon, Malaysia, and southern and southeastern Asia. The mixed-race descendants of these early residents would later be labeled "colored" people by the Afrikaners. In addition to importing slaves, the VOC released some of its employees from their labor contracts. These people quickly spread out from Cape Town to establish their own farms. The free burghers expanded their landholdings by stealing pastureland from the locals. The Khoi rebelled in 1673, and a four-year war followed. However, the Khoi were no match for the Dutch, who possessed superior weapons. And the local population was further reduced in 1713 when 90 percent of the surviving Khoi in the region were killed in a smallpox epidemic unintentionally brought to the Cape on a Dutch ship.

A severe land shortage developed around Cape Town as the population continued to grow. About fifteen hundred European men, women, and children were living alongside an equal number of slaves. The white population consisted of Dutch and German settlers and several hundred French Huguenots (Protestants) fleeing persecution in

Catholic France. Whatever their ancestry, the Europeans who were not employed by the VOC were called Boers, the Dutch word for "farmers." They also referred to themselves as Afrikaners, to show that they lived independently from the VOC.

■ ■ ■ THE TREKBOERS

By the early eighteenth century, the Boers were settling the lands north and east of Cape Town and along the southwestern coast of the Cape Flats. Those leading the Afrikaner expansion were known as trekboers, meaning "hiking farmers." As their name implies, the trekboers did not live in permanent homes. They roamed the countryside in ox wagons and lived in tents while searching for grazing lands for their cattle. Often they were accompanied by their families and a few slaves who worked as herdsmen. The farming practices of the trekboers were little different from those of the Khoi. They grazed their cattle in an area until the grass was gone and then moved on to greener pastures. Oftentimes the old pastures were set on fire, allowing ashes to fertilize the land, which helped the grass to return.

While wandering through the grasslands, the trekboers often clashed with the San and the surviving Khoi. The result was constant warfare between blacks and whites. The Europeans often moved into an area and seized the springs and rivers the tribes depended upon. In retaliation, the indigenous peoples raided trekboer herds and stole cattle. During these clashes, hundreds of men, women, and children were wounded or killed.

■ ■ ■ AN INDEPENDENT REPUBLIC

Despite the wars, the Cape Colony continued to grow throughout the eighteenth century. By 1750 it had twenty thousand European residents along with twenty-five thousand slaves. They tended large Boer wheat fields and vineyards established by the French. In addition, about fifteen thousand Khoi and mixed-race people occupied the region. Whatever their background, these people were not directly governed

This twentieth-century illustration shows a typical eighteenth-century South African vineyard, or wine estate.

by the nations of Europe as were other African colonies. Instead, the VOC exerted firm control over Cape residents. Wealthy company officials and a few powerful free burghers dominated society. Most other Afrikaners worked as traders, innkeepers, and artisans such as blacksmiths, wheelwrights, brewers, bakers, and tailors.

In the outer reaches of the colony, the trekboers lived by their own rules. They were extremely hostile toward the indigenous people, whom they considered inferior savages. Slaves worked under a harsh regime, and they were tortured and killed if they resisted orders. When problems arose with the free San or Khoi, the trekboers raised small armies and dealt with them brutally.

While the trekboers were able to subdue the indigenous Africans in the area, their expansion was limited in several ways. The arid regions about 350 miles (563 km) north of the Cape Colony were too dry to

In the early nineteenth century, a few powerful men (called burghers in Dutch) controlled most of South Africa's wealth, while most of society was made up of poor whites and slaves. In 1803 German visitor Henry Lichtenstein described the massive estate owned by one of these burghers, Jacob Laubscher, who lived 80 miles (129 km) north of Cape Town:

> [The] stock of the farm consisted of eighty horses, six hundred and ninety head of horned cattle, two thousand four hundred and seventy sheep, and an immense quantity of poultry of all kinds. The family itself, including masters, servants, Hottentots [Khoikhoi], and slaves consisted of a hundred and five persons. . . . It will be seen that an African farm may almost be called a State in miniature. . . . From the produce of the lands and flocks must the whole tribe be fed, so that the surplus is not as great as might be supposed at first sight.

graze cattle. And 450 miles (724 km) east of Cape Town, a large group of Bantu-speaking Africans called the Xhosa had established a large settlement on the Great Fish River. This population was swelled by runaway slaves and Khoi who found welcome refuge among them.

The Xhosa had been trading with the trekboers for decades, exchanging cattle and ivory for Dutch products such as nails, beads, copper, brandy, and tobacco. However, in the late 1770s, peaceful relations broke down when the Xhosa population moved west of the

Great Fish River. During the same period, the trekboers were pushing east with their large herds of cattle. Between 1779 and 1793, conflict over land and water rights led to a series of frontier wars. People were killed, property was destroyed, and large herds of sheep and cattle changed hands. The trekboers were unable to establish dominance over the Xhosa. They blamed their losses on a lack of support from the VOC. The bitter feelings led to a trekboer rebellion in the Graaff-Reinet region in 1795, and the Afrikaners founded an independent republic there.

THE BRITISH ARRIVE

The Dutch rebellion around Graaff-Reinet became a minor matter when the British took over the Cape settlement in 1795. The British, at war with the French emperor Napoléon, were worried that the strategic port might fall into French hands.

By this time, British trade in the East Indies surpassed that of the Dutch. Great Britain was firmly committed to maintaining its sea route to India.

British troops were sent east from Cape Town and easily quelled the trekboer revolution. But like the VOC, the British at first had little desire to become involved in a frontier battle between the Afrikaners and the Africans. To prevent further problems caused by an expanding Dutch population, the British restricted European immigration and relied instead on imported slaves and low-wage indigenous labor.

To control the black population, the British instituted the Hottentot Code of 1809. It required all free blacks (mainly the Khoi workers) to carry passes at all times stating where they lived and for whom they worked. Those caught without the passes could be sold to whites and forced into slavery.

The British soon found it impossible to ignore local problems. Ongoing battles between the Xhosa and the trekboers in the eastern region called the Zuurveld, or "sour grassland," required the British army to intervene repeatedly. The British soldiers mercilessly slaughtered the Xhosa in three different military actions before 1819.

In the aftermath, surviving Xhosa were removed from their traditional homeland along the Great Fish River. To prevent the Xhosa from reentering the area, Great Britain paid British citizens to settle in the South African colony. About five thousand British men, women, and children moved to Africa. Each was given a 100-acre (40-hectare) plot of land that formerly belonged to the Xhosa.

■ ■ ■ POLITICAL RIGHTS FOR ALL

While the British Army dealt harshly with the Africans in the east, the colonial governors took a different approach to those living around Cape Town. In 1807 the British parliament outlawed British participation in the slave trade. This ended the main source of free labor in southern Africa. In the decade that followed, British missionaries began traveling to Cape Town in large numbers to convert the indigenous people to Protestantism. The missionaries worked to change the Hottentot Code and reign in the brutal slave labor practices of trekboers. In 1823 the government of Cape Town established laws to regulate slave labor practices. The Hottentot Code was amended to create minimum standards for providing food and clothing. It also limited the number of hours slaves could be forced to work. Within a few years, the law was broadened to restrict the right of owners to punish slaves. It also required slave owners to record punishments in special books that local officials could inspect. A panel called the Protector of Slaves was established to regulate the new laws.

The missionaries continued to exert a spirit of liberalism and promote tolerance toward Khoi and those called free persons of color. In 1828 the Cape government issued Ordinance 50. It abolished the Hottentot Code. As the ordinance said, nonwhites would no longer be forced to carry passes or forced to enter labor contracts.

> [No] Hottentot or other free person of colour lawfully living in this colony shall be subject to any forced service which does not apply to others of His Majesty's subjects, nor to any hindrance, interference, fine or punishment of any kind.

The ordinance did not regulate the treatment of slaves, but in 1834, slavery was outlawed in the British Empire. This meant that Cape Colony slaveholders were forced to give up their human property. Parliament compensated the slaveholders by paying them one-fifth of the value of their slaves. The former slaves were not compensated for their labor but were given large reserves where they could farm. Many of these were on the eastern frontier where the freed slaves could act as a buffer between hostile Xhosa and white settlers.

More rights were granted to the nonwhite population in 1836, when Africans were allowed to vote for municipal boards in towns and villages. Parliament ordered this change with the declaration, "Her Majesty's subjects must have political rights enjoyed by all alike." However, Cape attorney general William Porter expressed a

A wagon train carries Protestant missionaries into the South African interior in the 1830s.

more practical reason for granting the vote: "I would rather meet the Hottentot at the [ballot box] voting for his representative than in the wilds with his gun upon his shoulder."

■ ■ ■ THE GREAT TREK

Most trekboers viewed the new British policies as treachery and made plans to leave the colony. Beginning in 1836, about six thousand people of Dutch descent traveled north by ox wagon into the Highveld interior above the eastern Cape frontier. Although this was not an organized movement, it was later referred to as the Great Trek by Afrikaner historians. The participants in the Great Trek were called Voortrekkers, or pioneers. One of the leaders of the Great Trek was Piet Retief. In 1874 his sister Anna Steenkamp explained what motivated the Dutch de-

Piet Retief was one of the leaders of the Great Trek of the 1800s. In this journey, Dutch settlers fled the Cape Colony, where slavery had become illegal.

parture: "[Slaves] were placed on an equal footing with Christians contrary to the laws of God and the natural distinction of race and colour, so that it was intolerable for any decent Christian to bow down beneath such a yoke; therefore we ... withdrew in order to preserve our doctrines of purity."

Some Voortrekkers moved onto pastureland in the Natal region between the Orange and Vaal rivers. The area was the kingdom of the Zulu tribe led by a powerful king named Dingane kaSenzangakhona. Other whites moved farther north beyond the Vaal River where the Ndebele tribe had lived for centuries. As had happened in previous years, the Afrikaners came into conflict with the local Africans while competing for water, pastureland, and game. This resulted in a series of clashes that led to a bloody war between the trekboers and the Zulu.

The conflict started after Piet Retief bargained with Dingane to give Zulu lands to the Afrikaners. Dingane betrayed Retief and his party of sixty-six trekboers and had them murdered. The Zulu king then commanded his warriors to kill all Boers who entered Natal. This resulted in the death of another 540 Afrikaners. The Afrikaners retaliated by killing thousands of Zulu in the decisive Battle of Blood River. After this 1839 victory, the Afrikaners were able to establish the Voortrekker Republic of Natalia, or Natal Republic, along the coast of the Indian Ocean beyond the eastern Cape. The trekboers spread out throughout the republic and established farms on pasturelands that had been part of Zulu lands for generations.

Trekboers including Piet Retief lay down their weapons to enter the village of Zulu king Dingane kaSenzangakhona in 1838. The Zulu would subsequently execute all sixty-six trekboers. This engraving was created in the nineteenth century.

The mass slaughter of Zulu warriors in December 1838 proved to be a decisive victory for trekboers in Natal (*below, in a nineteenth-century illustration*). To avenge the death of Piet Retief and his party at the hands of Zulu warriors, Afrikaner leader Andries Pretorius formed a small army of 470 fighting men and 100 servants. The group traveled to the banks of the Ncome River to confront the Zulu. In preparation, Pretorius placed sixty-four wagons side by side in a circle overlooking the river. Cannons were placed in the openings between the wagons. At dawn on the morning of December 16, fifteen hundred Zulu warriors attacked the formation as the Afrikaners fired repeatedly from their cannons. After four separate charges, the Zulus finally retreated, leaving at least thirty-five hundred dead behind. Only three members of the Pretorius guard were slightly wounded. So many Zulus were killed that the river ran red with the blood, and it was renamed Blood River. The Afrikaners celebrated by claiming that their victory was proof of God's intervention and proof of their divine right to occupy the Natal. The victory at Blood River is still celebrated every year on December 16 by Afrikaners.

A government center was established. The governing body of Natal, called the Volksraad, quickly passed a series of laws to keep the races separate. All nonwhites, except slaves and those working for white people, were ordered to leave Natal. The remaining black and mixed-race people, referred to in Afrikaans as *skepsels* or "creatures," were not permitted to own land, horses, or firearms. They could not move about without permits signed by whites.

The Republic of Natal did not last long. The British governors of the Cape Colony felt threatened by an independent Dutch-speaking republic. They annexed (took over) the region in 1843. They changed the name to the Natal Colony and proclaimed that there would be no legal distinction between whites and blacks. This forced the majority Voortrekkers to move once again and return to the Highvelt. The hostility generated by the British annexation of Natalia further divided the Cape into separate, hostile groups. The interior became almost exclusively Afrikaners, while the populated coastal region became a typical British colony. English was the official language, used by government agencies and taught in schools. Although the white population of the Cape Colony shared a common European heritage, they spoke different languages and practiced different social and religious customs. Among the British, the term "Boer" was used in a derogatory manner. The rivalry between the Dutch and British cultures added another element to an already complex society divided along ethnic and racial lines.

■ ■ ■ A DANGEROUS DIAMOND MADNESS

Whatever its problems, until the mid-1860s, the Cape Colony remained an undeveloped agricultural outpost largely ignored by the rest of the world. But in 1866, a young shepherd named Erasmus Stephanus Jacobs picked up an odd-looking white pebble along the banks of the Orange River near where it joins the Vaal River. The boy's neighbor showed it to a traveling trader, who took it to the nearest geologist 200 miles (322 km) away in Grahamstown. The geologist was astounded to discover that the stone was a massive 21-carat diamond. The stone, called the Eureka, was purchased for five hundred pounds by Philip Woodhouse, the colony governor. To the average white South African worker, that sum was equal to nearly half a million dollars.

Three years after Eureka was discovered, diamond diggers found large stones at several nearby farms. The area was in the independent Boer nation, the Orange Free State, located between the Orange and Vaal rivers. In 1871 an 83.5-carat diamond was found in the area, setting off a diamond rush, or

In 1866 the Eureka diamond became the first diamond discovered in South Africa. It led to a diamond rush in the Orange Free State. This photo shows the diamond in its cut form.

what one Cape Town newspaper called "a dangerous madness." Diamond fever gripped the colony. Shopkeepers closed their shops, tradesmen threw down their tools, and sailors abandoned their ships in the harbor.

Driven by the dream of sudden wealth, several thousand men set off on horseback, in ox wagons, and on foot 550 miles (885 km) across the Great Karoo scrublands to the diamond diggings. They congregated in a town called New Rush, which was renamed Kimberley in 1873. By this time, South African diggers had been joined by a motley bunch of fortune hunters from Australia, the United States, England, Ireland, and Germany. The population around Kimberley soared to twenty thousand whites and thirty thousand blacks.

In the early years of the discovery, workers with picks and shovels uncovered a vast wealth of precious stones. Some lucky diggers found ten or twenty diamonds before breakfast. One impoverished Englishman discovered a 175-carat stone valued at the astounding sum of thirty-three thousand pounds (about $5 million in 2010). However, the easy finds were soon exhausted and miners were forced to live in a harsh environment with little hope of striking it rich. The nearest water was 20 miles (32 km) away, open trenches were used as latrines, clouds of flies swarmed on everything, and sudden blinding dust storms ripped tents from the ground. With burning hot days and bitter, cold nights, the diamond digs around Kimberley quickly earned a reputation as a place of dysentery, drunkenness, and poverty.

The diamond rush would have ended as quickly as it started. But geologists discovered that the gems found at the surface were outcrops of diamond-laden volcanic pipes that went deep into the ground. Scientists soon realized that the dry, dusty desert of the Orange Free State contained the largest concentration of diamonds in the world.

■ ■ ■ "THEY MUST BE TREATED AS CHILDREN"

Like many other major events in the Cape Colony, the discovery of diamonds only served to increase tension between the competing groups of Dutch, British, and nonwhite citizens. The British government seized control of the digging despite Voortrekker claims to the land. Four mines were developed. Within a decade, Kimberley grew to be the largest city in the southern African interior. The massive growth of the diamond industry was made possible through the exploitation of poorly paid black laborers.

The diamond boom attracted up to fifty thousand Africans each year throughout the 1870s. Most worked for white diggers who controlled small claims. Wages were extremely low, but it was easy to steal diamonds because of their small size. Black laborers who smuggled diamonds were able to sell them to white diamond buyers, called touts, who operated out of the hundreds of sleazy bars in Kimberley. But although an estimated one-third to one-half of the diamonds were sold secretly in Kimberley, black diamond smugglers were mercilessly flogged (whipped) or even lynched if they were caught. The touts were not treated as harshly. They were run out of town, and their property was taken.

In addition to diamond theft, white miners were upset by the competition posed by black African and mixed-race claim holders. Angry miners threatened rebellion unless the government intervened to regulate nonwhite workers. The British responded by passing Proclamation 14 in August 1872. The declaration referred to African and mixed-race workers as "servants" and whites as "masters." It required a servant to carry a pass signed by his master. Those caught without a pass could receive a three-month prison sentence or be subjected to flogging. If a master suspected a servant of diamond theft, the master was entitled to search the residence, property, or even the body of the suspect.

Proclamation 14 spelled out the official attitude toward the colony's black workers. It referred to them as "Kaffirs," a derogatory term used at the time to describe black people of southern Africa: "[The] great mass of the labouring coloured population consists of raw Kaffirs, who

Thousands flocked to the Kimberley diamond mines in the 1870s. The rush became an industry when diamond-laden volcanic pipes were found.

come from the interior with every element of barbarism, and no touch of civilization among them; in fact they must be treated as children incapable of governing themselves."

The year Proclamation 14 was passed, the Cape Colony was celebrating its 220th anniversary. But nearly every one of those years was marked by bitter struggle. Whether the battles were over cattle, pastures, water, or diamonds, nearly every conflict centered on race and ethnic background. While many quarrels were between the British and Afrikaners, the biggest losers were always the Zulu, San, and Khoi people who had occupied the region for thousands of years.

CHAPTER 2

REMARKABLE **RICHES** AND **RACIAL** INTOLERANCE

"We must find new lands from which we can easily obtain raw materials and at the same time exploit the cheap slave labor that is available from the natives of the colonies."

—Cecil John Rhodes, founder of De Beers Consolidated Mines, 1882

In the 1880s, the diamond mines surrounding Kimberley were driving the economic fortunes of the Cape Colony.
Money from the valuable gems paid for development and brought great wealth to a small portion of the Cape's white population. No one benefited from the diamond trade more than Cecil Rhodes, a British-born former fruit farmer. Rhodes moved to Kimberley shortly after diamonds were discovered in 1871. He made money renting equipment to miners, using his profits to buy up all available diamond claims. Rhodes founded De Beers Consolidated Mines. The company gained almost total control of the entire diamond industry by the end of the 1880s.

Diamonds made Rhodes the richest man in Africa. Like many Europeans before him, he felt the need to exert total control over the lives of his African workers to maintain his empire. To achieve this, Rhodes sponsored a law called the Diamond Trade Act. This law, enacted in 1882, was meant to deal with diamond theft. Rhodes

Cecil Rhodes *(fourth from left)* became the richest man in Africa through the diamond industry and his company, De Beers Consolidated Mines.

Diamond miners for De Beers work at the bottom of the great shaft at the Wesselton Mines, Kimberley, South Africa, in 1911.

called this the ultimate evil. Since diamonds were small and easy for workers to smuggle out of the mines, the Diamond Trade Act put in place a system that would restrict and segregate (separate) the nonwhite citizens of the Cape for more than one hundred years.

DIAMOND DETENTION CENTERS

The Diamond Trade Act called for a maximum fine of one thousand pounds (about $12,000 in 2010) and a prison term of fifteen years for those convicted of possessing stolen uncut diamonds. Suspects were guilty until proven innocent, and a special court was set up to try accused thieves. Police were given powers to search a person and his property without a warrant. A special police unit was set up to entrap potential diamond thieves.

Despite the harsh measures, diamond smuggling continued. In reaction, Rhodes worked for an amendment to the Diamond Trade Act in 1883. The new regulation required black mine workers to wear uniforms and to strip naked in buildings called search houses when they entered or left the mines. The indignities were described on the ANC website, "Africans were searched every day at the end of their shift. Stripped naked, they jumped over bars and paraded with arms extended before guards, who scrutinized hair, nose, mouth, ears and rectum with meticulous care. It was much the same kind of search that Africans endured in Kimberley's central prison."

The prison model was no accident. Rhodes intended to convert the De Beers mines into detention centers. Rather than search workers every day, African miners, called inmates by the company, were confined to an enclosed compound for four to six months at a time. Conditions were described by De Beers general manager Gardner Williams in 1902:

> Four acres [1.6 hectares] are enclosed, giving ample space for the housing of its three thousand inmates, with an open central ground for exercise and sports. The fences are of corrugated iron, rising ten feet [3 meters] above the ground. . . . Iron cabins fringe the inner side of the enclosure, divided into rooms 25 feet by 30 feet [8 by 9 m], which are lighted by electricity. In each room twenty to twenty-five natives are lodged.

The living conditions, which continued well into the twentieth century, were degrading. But even more degrading was the treatment of workers who left the grounds. Before being discharged, the men were confined in open detention rooms for several days. They were stripped naked and wore nothing but blankets. Their hands were put in fingerless gloves that were padlocked to their waists. This was done to prevent the miners from concealing stolen diamonds in cuts, wounds, or body orifices. The workers were forced to drink purgatives, which made them evacuate their bowels. Their waste was closely examined for swallowed diamonds.

HOLDING FIRMLY TO TRUTH

Nonwhite residents of the Cape Colony who wanted to earn a living had to submit to humiliating and degrading racist laws. Nonwhite visitors to the colony were often shocked by the official racism that governed nearly every aspect of daily life. One of those visitors was Mohandas Karamchand Gandhi, a twenty-four-year-old lawyer from India. In 1893 Gandhi visited the city of Durban in Transvaal Province to represent a client in a lawsuit. He was the first nonwhite lawyer allowed to argue a case in a Transvaal courtroom.

Several weeks after his court date, Gandhi needed to take a business trip to the capital city of Pretoria in the Natal Colony. He bought a first-class ticket, but when his train entered the station at Pietermaritzburg, a white city, he was ordered to move into a third-class train car. Gandhi was told by a police officer that he could not travel in the first-class

Mohandas Gandhi *(seated center)* and his staff pose in front of his law office in South Africa in the early 1900s.

compartment because he was not white. When Gandhi refused to move, he was thrown off the train on a rainy, bitterly cold evening. Gandhi was forced to spend the night in a frigid "coloured-only" waiting room in the nearly empty train station. The next day, he had to complete his journey by stagecoach, where he suffered further humiliations as a second-class citizen. As a native of India, Gandhi was barred from hotels and restaurants and forced to give up his seat to a white passenger.

Gandhi would go on to help India gain independence from Great Britain in the 1930s and 1940s. But the humiliating experiences in Transvaal made him question his status in the world for the first time. This exposure to segregation inspired him to change the direction of his life. After a few weeks observing the conditions of the Indian population of Pretoria, Gandhi decided to stay in the Cape Colony and work for change. He called together of group of Indian residents, and they decided to form a political party, the Natal Indian Congress (NIC), to fight discrimination.

In 1896 Gandhi started a battle against South African discrimination that would last more than two decades. He began by teaching the Indian population techniques of passive resistance against Afrikaner discrimination. Gandhi coined the term *satyagraha* to describe his political philosophy. *Satyagraha* is taken from the Sanskrit words "truth" and "holding firmly to." In his own words, Gandhi describes the satyagraha philosophy of nonviolent resistance:

> Truth (satya) implies love, and firmness (agraha) . . . serves as a synonym for force. I thus began to call the Indian movement 'Satyagraha,' that is to say, the Force which is born of Truth and Love or non-violence.

THE BOER WAR

By the time Gandhi was working with the Natal Indian Congress, a second industrial revolution was well under way about 270 miles (435 km) northeast of Kimberley. It began in 1886, when huge gold deposits were found in the hills of the Witwatersrand range, an area called the

Rand. The discovery led to the Boer War, one of the bloodiest conflicts in Cape history.

The Rand was sparsely populated, but the discovery set off a gold rush. More than one hundred thousand people, about half of them white Europeans, flocked to the area. The influx turned the dusty settlement of Johannesburg into a bustling boom town practically overnight. Within a decade, nearly one-fifth of all gold production in the world was taking place on the Rand. The gold mines employed five times more nonwhite workers than the diamond industry.

The Rand was located in a Boer-ruled country called the South African Republic. Until gold was discovered, the British had little interest in the region. But as the nineteenth century ended, Great Britain was in desperate need of funds to pay for its empire, which stretched

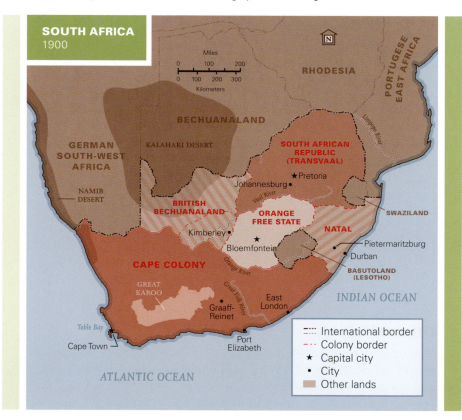

Anyone studying a map of southern Africa will notice a small landlocked country in the middle of South Africa. This is the Kingdom of Lesotho, home to 1.8 million people. The kingdom was founded by the Bantu king Moshoeshoe I in 1822 and originally named Basutoland. During the Great Trek of 1836, Afrikaner trekboers began arriving in Basutoland and attempted to colonize the region. In the following decades, Afrikaners from the bordering Orange Free State clashed with Moshoeshoe in a long-running dispute known as the Free State-Basotho Wars. After fighting a series of losing battles with the Afrikaners, Moshoeshoe successfully petitioned the British to intervene. Basutoland was made a British protectorate in 1868. The kingdom gained its independence from Britain in 1966 and was renamed the Kingdom of Lesotho.

from India to the Caribbean. The gold in the hills east of Johannesburg was seen as a perfect remedy to Britain's money woes.

In 1899 a British fleet set sail for southern Africa carrying nearly one-half million men, a number equal to the entire Afrikaner population. The army was under orders to take the South African Republic from the Boers. They quickly captured Johannesburg and Pretoria, about 40 miles (64 km) to the north. However, Afrikaner guerrillas, with their intimate knowledge of the countryside, were able to slaughter British troops, blow up railroads, and cut lines of communication. The British reacted with a vicious scorched earth policy. They burned farms, churches, and villages to the ground and poured salt into the fields so crops could not be grown again. Thousands of Afrikaner men, women, and children were herded into concentration camps, where many died.

Top: Boer civilians wait in a British concentration camp during the Boer War (1899–1902).
Bottom: Indian workers brought to South Africa as cheap labor plant sugarcane at a plantation in the Natal in the early 1900s.

The British declared victory in the renamed Transvaal in 1902, but the death toll was high. About twenty-eight thousand Afrikaners, more than half the population, died along with twenty thousand British troops. And although the Boer War was fought between European groups, Africans served on both sides. Their contributions received little acknowledgment. About twenty thousand nonwhites were killed in the conflict.

THE ASIATIC REGISTRATION ACT

The British fought the Boer War to take control of the Cape's gold. Great Britain was little interested in changing the racist attitudes of the Afrikaners because they did not want to touch off another bloody war. The British government did not protest when the Transvaal legislature, led by Afrikaner Louis Botha, enacted a law called the Asiatic Registration Act.

The Asiatic Registration Act required all so-called Asiatics, people of Indian and Chinese descent, to provide a thumbprint and personal details to the government for registration. Anyone who failed to do so would not be granted the right to trade in the Transvaal. The law applied only to men. Those without a registration certificate could be fined immediately or deported (sent home) without a trial.

The law threatened the livelihoods of male Asians. But Gandhi noted that it was also humiliating since only criminals were required to give their thumbprints in most countries. At a mass protest on September 11, 1906, Gandhi urged his followers to practice satyagraha and defy the law. The protesters vowed to face arrest rather than agree to the demands of government authorities. In the months that followed, Indians fought the registration act through nonviolent resistance—holding strikes, demonstrations, and protest marches. The government reacted by jailing thousands, including Gandhi. Some were flogged, and a few were shot.

The violent reaction to the peaceful satyagraha protests was condemned in India and Great Britain. The negative public attention finally forced Transvaal interior minister Jan Smuts to negotiate a compromise with Gandhi and the Natal Indian Congress. In the deal, Indians would voluntarily register, but the law would be repealed by the legislature. To show good faith in the bargain, Gandhi himself was the first to register.

Despite the compromise, Smuts failed to live up to his word and the law was not repealed. The Natal Indian Congress reacted by organizing strikes in coal mines and sugarcane fields, where most Indians worked. Mass protests were held, and people burned their registration cards. Some were arrested and sentenced to hard labor. Others were deported. Eventually, however, the Indians were victorious and the law was changed. This prompted Smuts to tell Gandhi:

> I often wish you took to violence like in English strikes, and then we would know at once how to dispose of you. But you will not injure even the enemy. You desire victory by self-suffering alone and never transgress your self-imposed limits of courtesy and chivalry. And that is what reduces us [the government] to sheer helplessness.

Gandhi *(fourth from left)* **and other resisters pose after being released from prison following a satyagraha protest in South Africa in 1908.**

■ ■ ■ THE ACT OF UNION

The troubles over the Asiatic Registration Act took place at a time when the Parliament was finding it increasingly difficult and expensive to govern the colony thousands of miles from London, England. Hoping to prevent another war, British and Afrikaner leaders enacted plans for statehood. In 1908 leaders from the four separate colonies, Cape, Natal, Transvaal, and the Orange Free State, held a national convention in Durban. Under the leadership of Smuts, the delegates voted to create the Union of South Africa with a centralized government. The colonies would become statelike provinces that were governed by province councils. Representatives from each council would meet in a Union parliament that would govern the new nation.

While the colonies wanted independence, major disagreements broke out at the national convention over racial issues. The Cape Colony allowed nonwhites to vote and serve in political office. In Natal, Transvaal, and the Orange Free State, the vote was limited to whites only. Delegates from Natal refused to enter into a union if it meant that black Africans and mixed-race people could make laws that would

govern white men. The Natal delegates threatened to walk out of the convention if the other colonies did not address the issue. In the end, it was decided that each province would be able to decide the issue itself. This meant that nonwhites would only be able to vote and run for office in Cape Province and only white men could serve in the Union parliament.

As its last act, the national convention drafted a constitution that was sent back to the four colonial legislatures for approval. Some lawmakers in the Cape tried to have the document changed to give voting rights to nonwhites, but they were defeated.

On May 31, 1910, the British parliament approved the Act of Union, and the four separate colonies were united to form the Union of South Africa. Louis Botha was named as the first prime minister. A census taken the following year showed the new nation had nearly 6 million residents. About 1.2 million South Africans were of European descent, more than 4 million were black Africans, and 677,000 were classified "coloreds"—

In 1910 a Boer preacher prays as part of the opening of the South African Union's first parliament session.

Indians, other Asians, and those of mixed race. Whites controlled South Africa and its great wealth of diamonds and gold. Yet the Europeans were outnumbered by nonwhites by more than three to one.

■ ■ ■ THE NATIVE LANDS ACT

When the Union of South Africa was formed, black Africans lived in various conditions depending on where they resided. In the former Orange Free State, black people lived on three relatively small parcels of land called reserves. In Natal the British set aside almost 4 million acres (1.6 million hectares) as reserves for Bantus, Zulus, and other African groups. In the Cape, Africans lived on parcels varying in size from a few acres to larger reserves set aside by the government. Africans also became migrant workers, temporarily occupying land owned by white farmers who employed them during planting and harvesting seasons. In addition, black Africans were able to buy or lease land everywhere but in the Orange Free State. Blacks owned more than 1 million acres (400,000 hectares) in South Africa.

In 1912, when James Barry Munnik Hertzog was

Two Zulu women work in a field in the early twentieth century. Opportunities for blacks were limited before the formation of the Union of South Africa and became worse once the new union was formed.

appointed minister of native affairs, he wanted to segregate property ownership in South Africa. Hertzog was a former general who commanded the Orange Free State military during the Boer War. He did not believe blacks and whites should live together.

Hertzog drafted the Native Lands Act. This law set aside 7.3 percent of South Africa's lands for black people, who made up 67 percent of the population. The remaining 92.7 percent of the land would be given to whites, who were about 24 percent of the population. Mixed-race people, about 9 percent of the nation's inhabitants, would be allowed to live among the whites.

James Barry Munnik Hertzog believed firmly in segregation of blacks and whites. He used his position as minister of native affairs to institutionalize the practice.

THE SOUTH AFRICAN NATIVE NATIONAL CONGRESS

The Native Lands Act classified all blacks as a single group culturally and socially. However, in the early twentieth century, South Africa's black population could be divided into five major groups. There were those who lived in the traditional tribal manner on reserves established before union. Others, called detribalized, were largely illiterate and worked mainly on farms. Another group of blacks lived in cities, where most adopted modern urban lifestyles. A smaller group of migrants came to South Africa from other parts of the continent to work in the mines. They returned to their native lands when their contracts expired. Educated blacks, from Christian schools, lived very much like Europeans in urban areas.

In January 1912, as the Native Lands Act was being debated in Parliament, a group of educated South Africans met in Bloemfontein in the Orange Free State to discuss resistance to the plan. The group was made up of clergy, lawyers, and educators, as well as clerks, servants, and tribal chiefs. The group was led by Pixley ka Isaka Seme, a member of the Zulu royal family. He had been educated at Columbia University in New York City before attending law school at Jesus College, Oxford University. Seme explained the purpose of the meeting:

> [In] the land of their birth, Africans are treated as hewers [cutters] of wood and drawers of water. The white people of this country have formed what is known as the Union of South Africa—a union in which we have no voice in the making of laws and no part in their administration. We have called you, therefore, to this conference so that we can together find ways and means of forming our national union for the purpose of creating national unity and defending our rights and privileges.

Pixley ka Isaka Seme was a Zulu royal who graduated from Columbia and Oxford universities. He helped form the SANNC in 1912 to fight for equality for blacks in South Africa.

After Seme's speech, the group voted to form a political organization, the South African Native National Congress (SANNC). (The name was shortened to the African National Congress, or ANC, in 1923.) The congress named renowned Zulu leader John Dube president-general. Like Seme, Dube was a member of the Zulu royalty and had been educated in the United States. A theologian and teacher, Dube was strongly influenced by the African American educator Booker T. Washington, who was the first president of Tuskegee College in Alabama. In South Africa, Dube set up a school for black Africans in Natal and published the colony's first African newspaper, *Illanga lase Natal* (Sun of Natal).

The goal of the SANNC was to use nonviolent means to gain equality for all South African blacks. To achieve this goal, the national constitution would have to be amended to remove what was called the color bar in education, industry, and government. To publicize the work of the SANNC, Seme founded the first national African newspaper, the *Abantu-Batho* (People). An unsigned editorial in the newspaper outlined the goals of the African congress: "We were dreaming of changes . . . of the day when Africans would sit in Parliament and would be able to buy land."

■ ■ ■ A BITTER SENSE OF WRONG

Despite protests from the SANNC and white liberals, the Native Lands Act was rushed through Parliament and became law on June 16, 1913. The following year, Dube and other members of the SANNC set sail for Great Britain to submit a petition to Parliament asking for help in

The SANNC delegation to Great Britain poses for a picture in 1914. President-General John Dube is in the center.

repeating the act. The Africans were given a cold reception. By the time they returned home, Great Britain had declared war on Germany, an act that marked the beginning of World War I (1914–1918). The problems of South African blacks would be of little concern to the British as they struggled for survival on the bloody battlefields of Europe. Acknowledging this, the SANNC passed a public resolution that said they decided "to hang up native grievances against the South African Parliament till a better time."

White South African soldiers were fighting side by side with the British. But when Dube offered to enlist five thousand black soldiers for the war effort, he received a stinging response from Smuts, who was minister of defense, "[The] government is anxious to avoid the employment of Coloured [or others not of European descent,] in warfare against whites." While the government would not allow blacks to be armed, 10,000 black laborers were recruited to dig trenches and perform menial labor in France. Before the war ended in 1918, 865 of the black South African laborers died in the conflict.

Ironically, as South Africans fought for democracy in Europe, the Native Lands Act was creating extreme hardships at home. The law, called the Black Lands Act, forced many migrant farmworkers off the land. Thousands took to the roads in the middle of winter, carrying their belongings on their heads, holding their children, and driving starving flocks of sheep. Dying carcasses littered the ditches. The secretary of SANNC, Solomon Plaatje, described the situation in the Orange Free State, "It looks as if these people are so many fugitives escaping from war."

As the squatters moved from one white farm to another begging for work or food, they realized that they could only survive by permanently moving to the already overcrowded reserves. Once they reached the reserves, the displaced farmers were forced to line up at the Native Labour Offices. Only the strongest and healthiest men were issued work permits. Those lucky enough to receive passes could then walk to Rand, where they would live in barracks and work in the gold mines.

The Black Lands Act forbade white farmers from leasing land to blacks. This provision hit those Africans, called bywoners, particularly hard. The bywoners had large herds of oxen and sheep and had done well ranching on leased land. As Plaatje wrote, the bywoners were "fairly comfortable, if not rich and enjoyed the possession of their stock, living in many instances just like Dutchmen." After being evicted, the bywoners were plunged into poverty.

Discussing the effects of the act on the bywoners and others, a 1914 article in the *Christian Express* stated the process was creating a "bitter sense of wrong in the Native mind." However, leading white politicians defended the act, saying it was enacted only to prevent friction between white and black cultures. Smuts, who served as minister of three departments—mines, interior, and defense—strongly defended the Black Lands Act in a 1917 speech:

> Instead of mixing up Black and White in the old way, confusing everything and not lifting up Black but degrading the White, we are now trying to keep them apart as much as possible in our institutions. In land ownership, in forms of government and in many ways we are trying to keep them apart and thus lay down the outline of a policy which . . . may in the end be the solution to our Native problem.

■ ■ ■ DEFYING AUTHORITY

By the time Smuts gave his speech, the SANCC had three thousand dues-paying members who did not see the Black Lands Act as a solution to their problems. And after the war ended, the group took measures to oppose the act using what it called peaceful propaganda (information to promote their cause) and passive actions. These moves were modeled on the satyagraha philosophy developed by Gandhi.

The first major action instituted by the SANCC took place in 1919. Thousands of protesters assembled in the Central Pass Office in Johannesburg to condemn the pass laws that had restricted nonwhites since the nineteenth century. Group members turned in their pass documents while singing the British national anthem, "God Save the Queen." While the action began as a peaceful event, police charged into the crowd and began beating protesters with batons. Those who had surrendered their passes were arrested. The violence sparked a riot, and seven hundred Africans were taken to prison.

In 1921 government forces took another action that proved the authorities were not about to tolerate any resistance, passive or not. In the rural east Cape town of Bulhoek, about five hundred members of a black religious sect, the Israelites, took over a plot of pastureland. They built a tabernacle (holy structure) to celebrate the Jewish festival of Passover. The group had done this for several years, building a temporary structure and moving on after the celebration. Then, in 1920, the group's leader, Enoch Mgijima, had a vision that the Israelites should permanently occupy the field. The government ordered the Israelites to move. When they refused, 800 heavily armed police officers were sent to evict the sect. When the sect members defied orders to disperse, authorities opened fire on the group, killing 171 worshippers and wounding 129.

The Israelites were part of a growing movement of resistance by religious sects in rural areas. They were among several groups that blended Judeo-Christian beliefs, tribal culture, and African separatist views. Because the groups were not centrally organized, local authorities dealt with them harshly. They only gained national attention after tragedies such as the Bulhoek massacre.

THE RAND REVOLT

Nine months after the Israelites were slaughtered, an armed conflict between white groups once again pushed aside the problems of nonwhites. And once more, gold was at the root of the crisis. Troubles began when gold prices steeply declined after World War I. To maintain their high profits, mining companies proposed replacing their semiskilled white workers with cheaper black labor. Driven by fears of unemployment, the white miners staged a strike that began on December 28, 1921. In the first protest march, militant Afrikaners marched through the streets of Johannesburg carrying banners that read "Workers of the World Unite, and Fight for a White South Africa."

A large crowd of striking miners gathers to listen to political speeches in Johannesburg on February 25, 1922. Strikers turn violent the next month, in what became known as the Rand Revolt.

White miners had organized strikes in previous years, but this rebellion was the most radical and violent in South African history. Angry English-speaking miners joined the Communist Party of South Africa (CPSA). They demanded the establishment of a workers' republic similar to that of the Soviet Union (fifteen republics that included Russia). On the other side of the political spectrum, Afrikaners organized their strike through the National Party (NP). This right-wing, whites-only political party was established by Hertzog in 1912.

Although the CPSA was composed of leftists and the NP was made up of rightists, the groups joined together in March 1922 to stage the Rand Revolt. What began as a strike escalated into an armed insurrection on the Witwatersrand. Armed revolutionaries took over the cities of Benoni and Brakpan and several Johannesburg suburbs.

Smuts, who had become prime minister, sent twenty thousand troops to break the rebellion. Working-class towns occupied by impoverished white miners were attacked by artillery, tanks, and bomber aircraft. More than 2,000 were killed, 4,748 were arrested, and 4 were hanged for their part in organizing the revolt.

■ ■ ■ THE "CIVILIZED LABOUR POLICY"

The miners' strike was followed by a period of economic depression as gold prices continued to slide. Widespread unemployment resulted in what was called "Poor White-ism." Government figures showed that three hundred thousand Afrikaners were living in poverty, near starvation. These people blamed Smuts for their problems. In 1924 the Afrikaners elected Hertzog to take his place as prime minister.

THE COMMUNIST MANIFESTO

English-speaking miners who were members of the Communist Party of South Africa hoped to establish a workers' republic similar to the Soviet Union. Members of the CPSA based their political philosophy on the *Communist Manifesto*, written in 1848 by German authors Karl Marx and Friedrich Engels. In the book, they write about average workers, called the proletariat, and their struggles with factory, mine, and farm owners, called the ruling class, or bourgeoisie. Marx and Engels argue that the proletariat should seize control of the means of production— all factories, farms, and mines. Under Communism, there would be no ruling class and everyone in society would be treated as equals. All Communist workers would share equally in profits generated by gold mines and other means of production.

In the 1920s, the social customs in Johannesburg, or Jo-burg (*below, in 1922*), were designed to humiliate blacks on a daily basis. Black Africans were not allowed to walk on the sidewalks. Instead, they had to navigate the muddy streets filled with animal waste. If a black man passed a white person, the black man had to remove his hat. Travel for blacks was restricted to fourth-class train cars that were originally designed to haul cattle. Police officers constantly stopped black people to examine their passes and other papers. Authorities raided black churches on Sundays to conduct document inspections. Those caught without the proper papers were immediately arrested. In the land they had inhabited for thousands of years, most black Africans were denied education, justice, and political representation.

> "Civilized labour is to be considered as the labour rendered by persons whose standard of living conforms to the standard generally recognized as tolerable from the usual European standpoint. Uncivilized labour is to be regarded as the bare requirements of the necessities of life as understood among barbarous and undeveloped peoples."
>
> —J. B. M. Hertzog, prime minister of South Africa, 1924

The election of James Hertzog as prime minister had ominous implications for black South Africans. True to form, Hertzog, the man who had written the Native Lands Act, introduced a series of laws (termed the civilized labour policy) that strongly favored the rights of white workers while denying even basic rights to blacks.

Hertzog was elected nearly forty years after gold was discovered on the Rand. While bringing great wealth to a handful of white South Africans, the massive gold deposits had done little to raise the general population out of poverty. Instead, gold drove a deep wedge between the races and allowed the government to rationalize the unjust treatment of the black majority. Rather than unite the country, gold was the cause of violence, nationalism, and racism. For black South Africans, the precious gold metal—associated the world over with glamour and the good life—was a heavy stone that dragged them down and destroyed their dreams of equality and respect.

CHAPTER 3

IMPLEMENTING
APARTHEID

"The Nationalist Government in its mad desire to enforce apartheid, has at every opportunity incited [led] the people to racial strife [conflict] and has attempted to crush their legitimate protests by ruthless police action."

—Dr. James Sebe Moroka, president-general of the
African National Congress, June 29, 1951

On July 18, 1918, a baby boy was born in the tiny village of Mvezo in the rural Transkei region of Cape Province, South Africa. The boy's great-grandfather, Ngubengcuka, had been a great monarch of the Thembu, a Xhosa-speaking tribe that once ruled the Transkei region. The baby's father, Henry Gadla, was part of the royal Thembu lineage. He was a relatively wealthy man married to four wives with whom he fathered thirteen children. The baby's mother, Fanny Nosekeni, was his father's third and favorite wife.

Gadla bestowed the name Rolihlahla on his youngest son. The name literally means "to pull a branch of a tree" but is more commonly used to mean "troublemaker." Perhaps Gadla could see into the future. When Rolihlahla grew up, he was known as Nelson Mandela. And he would live up to the name Rolihlahla by making a great deal of trouble for the apartheid government of South Africa.

When Mandela was nine years old, his father died of tuberculosis. The acting chief of the Thembu tribe, Jongintaba Dalindyebo, became the boy's guardian. Mandela moved to the chief's Great Palace in Mqhekezweni. By this time, Mandela was already a serious and studious boy. Although he was baptized into the Methodist Church, he was aware of his heritage as a descendant of the great Xhosa king. He understood that his culture required him to honor the memory of his ancestors by living a moral and righteous life. And as the first person in his family to attend school, Mandela also took an interest in his people's history. While he received a Western education at a mission school by day, at night he learned from tribal elders about the struggles of black South Africans. As the young Mandela understood it:

> [The] African people lived in relative peace until the coming of the *abelungu*, the white people, who arrived from across the sea with fire-breathing weapons. Once the Thembu . . . the Xhosa, and the Zulu were all children of one father and lived as brothers. The white man shattered the . . . fellowship of the various tribes. The white man was

hungry and greedy for land, and the black man shared the land with him as they shared the air and water; land was not for man to possess. But the white man took the land as you might seize another man's horse.

■ ■ ■ THE NATIVE BILLS

Mandela was learning his history lessons in a small town about 800 miles (1,287 km) east of Cape Town. But the peaceful atmosphere in Mqhekezweni stood in marked contrast to the social upheaval taking place in the capital city. This was a result of a number of "native bills" Hertzog enacted after he was elected prime minister in 1924. All of these laws had the effect of restricting the powers of black citizens.

While black male South Africans were still allowed to vote in Cape Province, Hertzog created a way to blunt their power in the electoral process. The Native Franchise Bill granted white women the right to vote for the first time. This effectively doubled the number of white voters, since black women did not have these rights. Another part of the bill denied blacks the right to serve in Parliament. Black males could only vote for white representatives.

While taking away black political representation, Hertzog moved to increase taxes on them. In 1925 a law was enacted to tax every male black African over the age of eighteen one pound (one hundred dollars) a year. In addition, all black African women and children had to pay a tax of ten shillings (forty-eight dollars). The only people who were exempt were those who were too sick to work. The taxes created severe hardships for the majority of black South Africans who lived in extreme poverty.

The Native Administration Act, passed in 1927, further eroded the rights of the black majority. It declared that the governor-general of each province, except the Cape, was the supreme chief of all blacks. This gave provincial governors far-reaching powers. They could immediately arrest and punish any black who defied a police order. Those who were seen as threats to peace and order, such as protesters or political organizers, could be held for up to three months without charges or trial. A black African could be so detained simply for speaking out against injustice, since the law contained a "hostility clause." This made "the uttering of any words, with the intent to promote feelings of hostility between Natives and Europeans" a crime. Those who violated the hostility clause could be imprisoned for one year, fined one hundred pounds, or both.

■ ■ ■ THE PAN-AFRICAN MOVEMENT

By the time Hertzog's native bills went into effect, the influence of the ANC had weakened. The group was poorly organized and had little money. In addition, many regarded the passive resistance tactics of the ANC as ineffective and viewed the group's leadership as an educated elite, out of touch with the common African. Most nonwhite South African activists belonged to the Industrial and Commercial Workers Union (ICU), which was established in 1919 as a trade union for dockworkers in Cape Town. The leader of the ICU, Clements Kadalie, was a mission-educated African from present-day Malawi. Throughout the 1920s, the ICU grew rapidly in both rural and urban areas as skilled and unskilled workers from industry and agriculture joined the union.

Most ICU organizers had ties to independent African churches. They had been influenced by Jamaican-born organizer Marcus Garvey. At that time, Garvey was living in New York City and leading a Pan-African movement. The Pan-African message preached black pride, self-reliance, and black solidarity. Garvey also promoted the Back to Africa movement. This was based on the idea that black people in the United States, the Caribbean, and the Americas should liberate Africa from the grip of white colonizers. In a 1919 speech at Madison Square Garden in New York City, Garvey told the cheering crowd:

It will be a terrible day when the blacks draw the sword to fight for their liberty. I call upon you blacks [of the world] to give the blood you have shed for the white man to make Africa a republic for the Negro.

Clements Kadalie *(left)* **and Marcus Garvey** *(right)* **were two leaders of the Pan-African movement in the 1910s and 1920s.**

Garvey's message of "Africa for Africans" was frightening to white South Africans. But many were also afraid of the Communist Party members who were working with the ICU. Many whites concluded the ICU was following orders from Soviet dictator Joseph Stalin, who considered Great Britain a capitalist enemy. Stalin openly stated he wanted to use South Africa's blacks to help bring down the British Empire. As Stalin told the CPSA in 1927, the black masses "are leaders in a revolutionary struggle . . . against the white bourgeoisie and the British imperialism. The Party should seek to weaken the influence of the [whites] . . . by developing peasants' [farmworkers'] organizations and spreading among them the influence of the Communist Party."

Kadalie had expelled CPSA members from the ICU in 1926. This did little to lessen the fears of South Africa's white leadership, especially as the organization continued to grow in popularity. By 1928 ICU membership included 200,000 Africans, about 15,000 mixed race, and 250 whites, making it a much larger political body than the ANC.

Leaders of the ICU demanded that whites give up their stranglehold on land ownership. Members also wanted political power to be shared between blacks and whites. However, the rural membership of the ICU was poor and isolated. Most could only take part in small local demonstrations that involved small actions such as livestock theft, work stoppages, and property destruction. Rather than promote the union's goals, these measures were simply looked upon as criminal acts by whites. The actions by rural ICU members also alienated urban workers who wanted backing to fight the white political and industrial power structure.

In the late 1920s, ICU split into two factions (groups): those who supported moderation and those who wanted militant action such as the violent overthrow of the government. Split in two, the ICU died out in the early 1930s. It did achieve several important goals, however. The ICU was the first black trade union in South Africa. More important, the union helped make its members aware of the Pan-African movement. It inspired young black activists as they continued to resist government repression in the decades that followed.

NAZI SYMPATHIZERS

While the black liberation movement stalled, the South African government continued to tighten restrictions against nonwhites. The worldwide Great Depression (1929–1942) further lowered gold and diamond prices, plunging at least one-third of the Afrikaner population into extreme poverty. The hungry, unemployed whites were moved by messages of radical nationalism and racial prejudice. During the 1930s, Adolf Hitler's National Socialist (Nazi) Party was ruling Germany and threatening to overrun other European nations. Hitler was strongly anti-Semitic. He spoke of killing all European Jews. After Hitler came to power in 1933, many South African political leaders, along with a large number of the Afrikaners, came under the influence of the Nazi Fascist movement. Much of the Afrikaner anti-Semitic fervor was directed at mineowners, many of whom were Jewish.

In Germany, Nazi commandos, called storm troopers, were also referred to as Brownshirts because of the uniforms they wore. In South Africa, Nazi sympathizers formed a militia (local military group) called the Grey Shirts. Many Grey Shirts gave political support to Daniel François Malan, South Africa's minister of interior, education, and public health. In 1934 Malan broke away from the Hertzog government and formed the Purified National Party, known simply as the National Party, or NP.

Despite strong support for the Nazis, South Africa was still a member of the British Commonwealth, a group of nations colonized by the British. When Great Britain entered World War II (1939–1945) against Germany, Hertzog's government provided support, men, and arms for the war effort. With a massive increase in production, Johannesburg faced a labor shortage. Africans began streaming into the city in record numbers for jobs.

ANTI-SEMITISM AND THE NATIONAL PARTY

D. F. Malan, founder of the National Party, was not only anti-black but also anti-Semitic. As a member of South Africa's parliament in 1937, Malan promoted the Aliens Act of 1937. The legislation was written after a few thousand German Jews moved to South Africa to escape Nazi persecution. The law prohibited the entry of any white immigrant who could not quickly become part of the white population, but it was squarely aimed at Jews. Discussing the Aliens Act of 1937, Malan told Parliament, "I have been reproached that I am now discriminating against the Jews as Jews. Now let me say frankly that I admit that it is so." Thousands who were denied entry into South Africa by the Aliens Act died. Six million Jews were killed in the Holocaust (mass slaughter) before the end of World War II in 1945.

Students study at Fort Hare University in the early 1940s. Nelson Mandela and many other future black leaders attended the college in Alice, South Africa.

MAKING TROUBLE

In 1940, as South Africa joined in the war effort, Nelson Mandela was completing his first year at Fort Hare University, a school that offered Western-style higher education to black Africans. During his freshman year, Mandela studied politics, Dutch law, English, anthropology, and native administration. Mandela also lived up to his name Rolihlahla at the school after becoming involved with the Students' Representative Council (SRC).

The SRC was the main student organization at Fort Hare. Students were required to elect six representatives to it each year. Before the election, however, a group of students met to discuss problems they had with school administrators. There were complaints about the food the school provided. The group also felt that the SRC was not independent but simply agreed to administration policies. The students, led by Mandela, decided to boycott the SRC election. The boycott worked. Only 25 students out of 150 voted. However, the small group that did vote elected Mandela as one of the six to serve on the SRC. Mandela refused to take the position because he did not feel the vote was valid. When the school's dean insisted he serve on the council or be expelled, Mandela chose to leave. He later studied for a law degree from the University of London External Programme.

■ ■ ■ ■ "ONE NATION OUT OF MANY TRIBES"

After quitting school, Mandela moved to Johannesburg, working for a short time as a guard at a gold mine. His friend and mentor, Walter Sisulu, helped him get a low-level job at a Johannesburg law firm. Sisulu was a member of the ANC and strongly believed that the organization would someday change the racial politics of South Africa.

Mandela joined the ANC in 1943. At the time, Anton Lembede, a lawyer, was a leading activist in the ANC. Lembede believed Africa belonged to Africans, who should demand the return of a land that was rightfully theirs. Heavily influenced by Marcus Garvey, Lembede criticized what he saw as the black inferiority complex that had been instilled by white society. He wrote, "The color of my skin is beautiful like the black soil of mother Africa."

Walter Sisulu was an ANC member and activist.

Although the ANC was the only large organization fighting for black rights, Lembede felt that group had become too moderate. Other young men in the ANC, such as Peter Mda and Oliver Tambo, felt the same way. In 1944 Mandela joined forces with these activist organizers to form the ANC Youth League (YL). The goal of the group was to plan a campaign of action that would attract major public support.

The Youth League was formed at a time when millions of black people

"I cannot pinpoint a moment when I became politicized, when I knew that I would spend my life in the liberation struggle. To be an African in South Africa means that one is politicized from the moment of one's birth, whether one acknowledges it or not. An African child is born in an Africans Only hospital, taken home in an Africans Only bus, lives in an Africans Only area, and attends Africans Only schools, if he attends school at all.

"When he grows up, he can hold Africans Only jobs, rent a house in Africans Only townships, ride Africans Only trains, and be stopped at any time of the day or night and be ordered to produce a pass, failing which he will be arrested and thrown in jail. His life is circumscribed [limited] by racist laws and regulations that cripple his growth, dim his potential, and stunt his life. This was the reality, and one could deal with it in a myriad of ways. I had no epiphany, no singular revelation, no moment of truth, but a steady accumulation of a thousand slights, a thousand indignities, a thousand unremembered moments, produced in me an anger, a rebelliousness, a desire to fight the system that imprisoned my people."

—Nelson Mandela, 1994

were moving to cities where jobs were plentiful because of the war effort. Many of these workers had experience in trade unions and other community organizations. They were quick to support the ideas of the Youth League, outlined by Mandela. "African nationalism was our battle cry, and our creed [belief] was the creation of one nation out of many tribes, the overthrow of white supremacy [rule], and the establishment of a truly democratic form of government."

Nelson Mandela *(far right)* and other ANC leaders attend a Youth League meeting in the early 1950s.

Although the Youth League's ideas were considered militant, events taking place overseas made members hopeful. While World War II was raging in Europe, British prime minister Winston Churchill and U.S. president Franklin Delano Roosevelt signed an agreement known as the Atlantic Charter. The document was a blueprint for Europe that would be put in place after the war. The charter promoted democracy, freedom from poverty and fear, and the right of the world's people to self-determination, or democracy. Churchill had no intentions of applying the goals of the Atlantic Charter to Africans. But it inspired the ANC to create a similar document called the African Claims Charter. It demanded full citizenship for all Africans, the right to buy and sell land, and called for the repeal of pass laws and other discriminatory legislation. Discussing the African Claims Charter, Mandela wrote, "We hoped that the government and ordinary South Africans would see that the principles they were fighting for in Europe were the same ones we were advocating at home."

THE NATIONAL PARTY TAKES CONTROL

The hopes Mandela and the ANC had for South Africa were dashed in the run up to the 1948 election. D. F. Malan was the candidate for prime minister in the revitalized National Party. Malan was running a campaign based on bitterness against the British and hatred of the nation's nonwhite population. The NP campaign strategy was to promote fear of African liberation, called the *swart gevaar*, or the "black danger."

Malan called his party's platform apartheid. It was the first time the word, which means "apartness," was used in a political sense. But apartheid described an old state of affairs in Africa, one that had changed little since the 1800s.

The NP was backed by the Dutch Reform Church. Religious leaders used the Bible to support the position that whites were God's chosen people and blacks were created to be servants. With overwhelming support from average Afrikaners, the Nationalists won the election. The victory shocked political analysts. They had expected Smuts to be reelected after helping defeat the Nazis. The victory also surprised ANC members. They did not even have a plan to oppose the NP, because the group never believed the Nationalists could win.

Within weeks of his victory, Malan formed the first all-Afrikaner government since the creation of South Africa in 1910. Still angry over their defeat in the Boer War and British political domination since that time, the NP purged (rid) the government of English-speaking bureaucrats. They enthusiastically began implementing a detailed program of apartheid based on the belief that whites were superior to nonwhites. The new laws would provide the government with extraordinary powers to thwart opposition by stifling free speech, demonstrations, and political resistance.

LAWS OF APARTHEID

Early moves by the Malan administration granted government control over the most personal decisions people made. The 1949 Prohibition of Mixed Marriages Act banned marriages between whites and all nonwhites, including mixed-race and Indian people. The Immorality

Act went further. It made any sexual relations between whites and nonwhites illegal.

Beyond personal relationships, the NP instituted a program of geographical separation on an unprecedented scale. The Native Lands Act of 1913 had long required special reserves for Africans, called Bantus by the NP. But in urban areas, people of all races lived side by side. The Group Areas Act of 1950 covered not only Africans but also those of mixed race and Indians. This law divided South Africa into separate areas for each race and forced people of different groups to move to government-approved reserves.

The beneficiaries of the Group Areas Act were poor whites who lived in integrated neighborhoods and wanted their nonwhite neighbors removed. If whites wanted nonwhite-owned land, homes, or businesses in a certain area, all they had to do was declare them white and take them. The biggest losers, once again, were urban Africans. They were forced onto rural reserves, where unemployment was high and living conditions much worse than in the cities.

The Group Areas Act was so disruptive that it was even condemned by an official government body called the Tomlinson Commission. After studying the effects of the act, the commission concluded that even under the best economic conditions, the areas set aside for Africans would support no more than two-thirds of the black population. The commission recommended that the government set aside more lands to Africans. But the Malan administration refused.

The very essence of apartheid, the act that allowed the government to implement its severe laws, was called the Population Registration Act of 1950. This law forced all South Africans to register by race. Their identity was stamped on their passes. To carry out this measure, the government set up race boards to decide if people were white, mixed race, or black. This law was particularly harmful to light-skinned, mixed-race people, who passed as whites. As Mandela writes, "[The areas] where one was allowed to live and work could rest on such absurd distinctions as the curl of one's hair or the size of one's lips." This form of racial classification caused more than one hundred thousand people who were formerly considered white to challenge

Police officers stop two men to check their passes as they travel to Johannesburg to work in the 1950s.

their classifications. Those who lost and were reclassified as mixed race lost their jobs, homes, and businesses. Some of these people who were married to whites found that their marriages were illegal, in violation of the Prohibition of Mixed Marriages Act and the Immorality Act. In addition, thousands of families were broken apart if some children passed as white while others with darker complexions did not.

A PROGRAM OF ACTION

Malan's government expected mass protests to apartheid and passed laws to prevent them. The first law was called the Suppression of Communism Act of 1950 (also called the Unlawful Organisations Act). This was aimed at the Communist Party of South Africa, which had been behind hundreds of earlier protests. The law made it a crime, punishable by ten years in prison, to belong to the CPSA. However, the Suppression of Communism Act went beyond banning the CPSA. It was broadly drafted to include any groups that might resist apartheid, including the ANC. The far-reaching act made it a crime to organize any mass resistance to government policy. The act banned any activities that brought about "political, industrial, social, or economic change within the Union by the promotion of disturbances or disorder." This clause allowed the minister of justice to name as illegal any political, trade, or social organization if members organized a strike or mass protest. If a group was deemed illegal, its members could have their movements restricted by an order from the justice ministry. This order banned them from taking part in gatherings, meetings, or public demonstrations.

Nonwhite trade unions were the first groups affected by the Suppression of Communism Act, since some union members did belong to the Communist Party. But members of the ANC Youth League did not believe the law would be applied to them. Mandela wasn't much concerned about the government's treatment of Communism because he viewed it as a foreign political philosophy dominated by whites. At the time, Mandela did not support the Communist idea that Africans were suppressed as an economic class. He believed blacks were oppressed because of the color of their skin. And ANC members were not interested in taking orders from Soviet dictator Joseph Stalin.

The Youth League had its own ideas for South African liberation when ANC met for its annual conference at Bloemfontein in 1950. The Youth League put forward a program of action based on Gandhian principles. The plan included boycotts, strikes, passive resistance, protest demonstrations, and short work stoppages called stay-at-homes.

Older members of the ANC were fearful. They refused to support the YL plan of action. However, the activists of the Youth League worked to defeat conservative members in the 1950 ANC election. Sisulu was elected secretary-general. Tambo and Mandela were appointed to the National Executive Committee. With Youth League members in executive positions, the ANC, for the first time, was moving in a radical and revolutionary direction.

■ ■ ■ A NATIONAL DAY OF PROTEST

Before the plan of action could be implemented, ANC YL leaders needed to reach an agreement about working with South Africa's Indian community. Mandela was against working with those he called "Indian shopkeepers and merchants." He was among many Africans who believed that the Indians exploited black labor. Sisulu, however, believed all South Africans, including blacks, liberal whites, Indians, mixed race, and Communists, were bound together in their opposition to apartheid. In the end, Sisulu's view won after the matter was put to a vote before the ANC executive council.

The ANC YL began planning its first mass action for June 26, 1950. The ANC National Day of Protest would be held with organizations including the South African Indian Congress (SAIC); the Communist Party of South Africa; and the African People's Organization, a mixed-race group.

Political protest was extremely difficult in South Africa. Strikes were illegal, there was no right to free speech, and the government controlled the physical movements of individuals. Those who were arrested for breaking the law could lose their jobs and their homes. Despite the difficulties of organizing a demonstration, Sisulu traveled around South Africa to speak with tribal chieftains, labor leaders, and community organizers.

On June 26, the ANC efforts were rewarded. In the cities, most nonwhite workers stayed off the job, while merchants refused to open their shops and businesses. In Eastern Transvaal, more than five thousand rural workers gathered for a demonstration. The strike was not as broad as leaders hoped. But it showed the Nationalists that people were not going to remain passive as apartheid was implemented.

■ ■ ■ POSTWAR CHANGES

The National Day of Protest was held at a time when South Africa was undergoing rapid change. World War II caused economic and social up-heavals that continued to influence postwar South Africa. Gold continued to generate about two-thirds of South Africa's revenues. At the same time, manufacturing expanded significantly to meet wartime demands.

On May 12, 1950, the National Executive Committee of the ANC called for a National Day of Protest with the following declaration:

1. Although the Unlawful Organisations Bill purports to be directed against Communism in general and the Communist Party of South Africa in particular, the ANC Executive is satisfied, from a study of the provisions of the Bill, that it is primarily directed against the Africans and other oppressed people, and is designed to frustrate all their attempts to work for the fulfillment of their legitimate demands and aspirations. The Bill is a further example of the determination of the white people of this country to keep the African in permanent subordination [kept as a lower class]. It goes without saying that the African people are equally determined that they are not going to remain in that position forever. The ANC is resolved to oppose this and other measures of a similar nature by all means at its disposal.

2. As a first step it was agreed to launch a campaign for a National Day of Protest. It is suggested that, on this day, to mark their general dissatisfaction with the position in this country, the African people should refrain from going to work, and regard this day as a day of mourning for all those Africans who lost their lives in the struggle for liberation.

As new factories opened and old ones hired more workers, the number of black people living in South African cities doubled.

By 1950 more Africans than whites lived in every South African city. Many lived in extreme poverty in undeveloped urban communities called townships on the outskirts of Cape Town, Johannesburg, and Durban. The townships, such as Soweto (outside Johannesburg) and Nyanga (outside Cape Town) lacked sewers and electricity. However, they also contained large numbers of people who were unhappy with apartheid. This allowed Mandela and others in the ANC to recruit new activists. While the white government had easily instituted apartheid, the growing urban black population was increasingly demanding official government recognition. With strikes and mass demonstrations, they were raising their voices in a nation where it was against the law to speak out and be heard.

CHAPTER 4

THE CAMPAIGN OF DEFIANCE

"Full democratic rights with direct say in the affairs of the government are the inalienable right of every South African—a right which must be realized now if South Africa is to be saved from social chaos and tyranny."

—Joint Planning Council of the African National Congress Defiance Campaign, March 1, 1952

In March 1952, Nelson Mandela acquired a driver's license so he could become a "one man taxi service" for the ANC. At the time, very few Africans could afford cars and few Youth League leaders could drive. But acting as ANC taxi driver was only one of many jobs Mandela took on to further the goals of the Youth League. He was also in charge of the busy office and spent most days on the phone talking to regional leaders coordinating league activities in different parts of the country.

Mandela felt great pride for his role in leading the 1950 National Day of Protest. But he was also learning that fighting an all-consuming battle against a powerful enemy had personal consequences. At the time, Mandela was married to Evelyn Mase, a nurse who was also from the Transkei district. The couple had their first child, a son, in 1946. A daughter, born in 1947, died at the age of nine months. In 1950 Mandela's second son, Makgatho, was born on June 26, the National Day of Protest. Mandela was at the hospital when the child was delivered. He soon had to rush off to carry out his duties as an executive of the Youth League. Several days later, Evelyn told Mandela that their first son, Thembi, asked her "Where does daddy live?" Mandela had been coming home so late and leaving so early in the morning that his son did not even realize that his father lived at home.

BANNED BY THE GOVERNMENT

Mandela missed his family, but he could not promise he would spend more time with them. The new event being planned by the ANC and the SAIC was not a one-day strike. The Campaign for the Defiance of Unjust Laws was meant to be an extended program of nationwide civil disobedience with the challenging goal of overturning apartheid.

Mandela started the campaign by drafting a letter to the South African prime minister in early February. He informed Malan that the ANC Youth League had used every legal and constitutional method available for fighting apartheid. Mandela said the ANC, the

SAIC, and other groups were prepared to conduct unlawful protests unless the government repealed the laws of apartheid by February 29. In conclusion, Mandela wrote, "The struggle which our people are about to begin is not directed at any race or racial group but against the unjust laws which keep in perpetual subjugation and misery vast sections of the population."

Malan's private secretary responded. He stated the administration's oft-repeated message that apartheid was beneficial to all South Africans, whatever their race. The secretary also informed Mandela that the ANC demands were not going to be considered:

> It should be understood clearly that the government will under no circumstances entertain the idea of giving administrative or executive or legislative powers over Europeans . . . to Bantu men and women, or to other smaller non-European groups. The government therefore has no intention of repealing the long-existing laws differentiating between European and Bantu.

The secretary concluded by warning the ANC that the full force of the government would be used to suppress any and all protests.

To stop the Defiance Campaign, the government used the Suppression of Communism Act for the first time. It issued banning orders against several members of the Communist Party and five members of the SAIC, including the president of the

Yusuf Dadoo was the president of the South African Indian Congress.

Congress, Yusuf Dadoo, who worked closely with Mandela and Sisulu. Being banned meant the activists would be forced to resign their posts. They could no longer attend meetings or take part in any protest activities. Dadoo and the others openly defied the banning orders and were arrested. They spent six weeks in jail while the Defiance Campaign was being organized.

A STRATEGY OF NONVIOLENCE

Undeterred by government threats, the ANC leadership split into two work groups to run the Defiance Campaign. The National Action Committee was created to supervise and coordinate the events that would take place throughout the country. The National Volunteer Board was formed to recruit and train volunteers. Mandela was chairman of both committees. But he put much of his energy into the volunteer board where his official title was volunteer in chief.

As volunteer in chief, Mandela was responsible for organizing the Defiance Campaign, canvassing for volunteers, and raising funds. He began his work in April, traveling throughout South Africa to recruit African, Indian, and mixed-race volunteers. He warned potential collaborators that they might be fired, arrested, or physically attacked. But volunteers were instructed not to retaliate with violence regardless of the actions taken by the police. Violent behavior would undermine the Gandhian principles driving the ANC campaign. However, as Mandela writes, he did not view Gandhi's satyagraha as a sacred principle but as a means to an end.

> If a particular method or tactic enabled us to defeat the enemy, then it should be used. In this case, the state was far more powerful than we, and any attempts at violence by us would be devastatingly crushed. This made nonviolence a practical necessity rather than an option.... The principle was not so important that the strategy should be used even when it was self-defeating, as Gandhi himself believed. I called for nonviolent protest for as long as it was effective.

AN ARMY OF FREEDOM

The Defiance Campaign was divided into two phases. The first was to be carried out by a small group of volunteers in urban areas. These protesters were instructed to enter "Europeans Only" train cars, waiting rooms, building entrances, parks, sports facilities, and other areas. They would also remain in white areas past curfew. The groups would be overseen by leaders who would inform authorities in advance when and where civil disobedience was going to take place. Planners believed that prior notification would lower the odds of police violence.

The second stage of the Defiance Campaign would take place when masses of nonwhite industrial workers walked out on strike. These actions were planned for in the weeks that followed the initial civil disobedience

Four days before the Defiance Campaign was set to begin, the ANC held a mass rally in Durban. About ten thousand people attended the demonstration, where they heard speeches by leaders of the ANC and the Natal Indian Congress. Some addressed the suffering common to

ANC supporters gather to protest apartheid at a rally in the 1950s.

most in the crowd as one unidentified activist stated:

> You who today work in the mines, you who today work on the farms, you who today build beautiful roads for the motor cars, you are the people who are hungry, you are the people who have no clothes, you are the people who must live under the pass laws, you are the people who are oppressed in this country. If they put you in jail I ask you: Is your condition any better outside?

Another unnamed speaker put forth more radical ideas, stating "I want to tell the White man that there are a hundred and fifty million of us in the continent of Africa . . . and only three million White people. When an army of freedom marches forward it will brush aside three million White people." Mandela was the keynote speaker, and looking out over the excited crowd, he announced, "We can now say unity between the non-European people in this country has become a reality."

A MATTER OF LIFE AND DEATH

Despite talk about an army of freedom, the Defiance Campaign began with small groups of people. They bravely and eagerly committed acts of civil disobedience with a sense that their deeds were making history. Volunteers who sat in the "Europeans Only" waiting room at the Port Elizabeth railway station were arrested without incident. Rather than fearing arrest, the defiers enthusiastically walked into waiting police vans loudly singing South African songs of freedom.

Mandela was in Boksburg on the morning of June 26. He was to deliver a letter to the local magistrate (judge) informing him about a civil action about to take place in the nearby township. Fifty volunteers were about to leave the township without permits.

When Mandela arrived at the magistrate's office, he was greeted by an army of photographers and reporters. After the letter was delivered, Mandela approached the gate where the demonstration was taking place. He said that from a half mile (0.8 km) away he could hear the

THE **MUSIC** OF **LIBERATION**

Whenever black South Africans gathered to protest, they were united in joyous, harmonious song. Their singing style emerged in Natal and is known by the name *isicathamiya*. This style consists of vocal music sung a cappella, or without instrumental backing. The style was developed by Zulu men who were forced to leave their home villages and live in large all-male dormitories while laboring in gold mines and factories. Separated from their wives and families, the men passed the time on Sundays (their only day off work) by participating in music and dance competitions that were judged by complex rules.

One of the most celebrated winners of the isicathamiya contests was Solomon Linda and his band the Original Evening Birds. Linda wrote robust singing of the fifty-three defiers and several hundred supporters.

The group was crowded around high metal gates that separated the township from the European neighborhood. The gates were locked, and nervous police stood on the other side. Sisulu was at the front of the defiers demanding that gates be unlocked. Behind him the Indian leader Nana Sita, though suffering from severe arthritis, enthusiastically urged the crowd to sing and chant. After a one-hour standoff, the gates opened and the volunteers surged through in violation of the pass law. The demonstrators were arrested and taken to the police station. When Sisulu appeared before a judge, he spoke to the courtroom, packed with reporters, government officials, and supporters:

> As an African, and national secretary of the African National Congress, I cannot stand aside in an issue which is a matter of life and death to my people. I wish to make this solemn vow and in full appreciation of the consequences it entails. As long

the song "Mbube," or "The Lion," in 1939. Known in the West as "Wimoweh," the song was a huge hit in the United States in 1950. It was used in the 1994 Disney animated film *The Lion King*.

During the 1950s, Mbube music was adopted by female vocalists who sang soaring five-part harmonies. Protest music was forbidden by the South African government. But Mbube singers often incorporated political slogans into their lyrics. The song "Azikwelwa," or "We Refuse to Ride," was about a bus boycott and was sung at protests. Mbube lyrics also incorporated chants such as "Free Mandela," a reference to Nelson Mandela, who was imprisoned for his political activities.

as I enjoy the confidence of my people, and as long as there is a spark of life and energy in me, I shall fight with courage and determination for the abolition [ending] of discriminatory laws and for the freedom of all South Africans, irrespective of colour or creed.

Mandela was not arrested at the initial Boksburg protest. He left at midnight, after attending a meeting of the action committee, wanting nothing more than a hot meal and a bed. Instead, he was greeted by a police officer, arrested, and taken to jail for violating the eleven o'clock curfew. Thrown in a cell with dozens of other defiers, Mandela spent several days planning new actions, singing, and discussing the movement with other prisoners.

OPEN THE JAIL DOORS

The first day of the Defiance Campaign was considered a rousing success. The volunteers followed instructions, there was no violence, and the protest was widely covered by reporters. In the following months, more than eighty-five hundred people defied authorities and went to jail often chanting "Hey, Malan! Open the jail doors. We want to enter." Most who were arrested were only held for a day or two although some remained imprisoned for several weeks. Fines rarely exceeded ten pounds (about four hundred dollars) and were often less.

The Defiance Campaign helped generate a fivefold increase in ANC membership. It jumped from twenty thousand to one hundred thousand. And acts of defiance spread from big cities to smaller towns and rural villages. Mandela was at the forefront of the movement, driving from province to province either late at night or very early in the morning to avoid police. In some villages, Mandela went door-to-door signing up volunteers and helping plan acts of defiance. This personal contact was necessary because very few poor South Africans had telephones or electricity for radios.

The Defiance Campaign was little more than four weeks old when South African authorities took measures to stop it. On July 30, 1952,

SLEGS BLANKE
EUROPEANS ONL

Volunteers take over a "Europeans Only" train traveling to Cape Town in 1952. They were taken from the train and arrested in Cape Town.

police conducted massive raids on ANC and SAIC offices. Officials also raided the homes of campaign leaders in Johannesburg, Kimberley, and Port Elizabeth. During their searches, police searched dozens of activists' homes and illegally confiscated (took) personal papers and official documents. More than 120 campaign leaders were banned from participating in public meetings.

Two weeks after the police raids, Mandela and twenty others, including Dadoo and Sisulu, were arrested and charged with high treason under the Suppression of Communism Act. The men were put on trial in early November, but the first day of the hearing attracted a large number of rowdy protesters, including groups of Indian schoolchildren. The demonstrators surrounded Johannesburg's main courthouse and filled the air with boisterous chants and songs. The courtroom was so loud that the trial could not proceed. The police admitted they were helpless, so the magistrate, Justice F. L. H. Rumpff, called on several defendants to go outside and calm the crowd. The protesters agreed to move to a nearby public park. There they listened to speeches by the defendants during a lunchtime recess.

After the initial excitement died down, the trial dragged on for several weeks. As expected, the government called on dozens of police officers to testify about the alleged crimes they had witnessed. One of the witnesses, a man known as Makanda, shocked the defendants when he appeared on the witness stand. Makanda was a well-known activist at ANC headquarters. He worked in Sisulu's office, performed janitorial duties, brought fish and chips for everyone in the office, and even offered to shine people's shoes. Makanda also played in a band

ANC president James Moroka *(top center)* tries to quiet the crowd outside the Johannesburg courtroom where antiapartheid leaders were being tried in August 1952.

that performed at a rally on the first day of the Defiance Campaign. But Makanda was a detective sergeant in South Africa's national security police force called the Special Branch. He had infiltrated (joined as a spy) the ANC, where he secretly wrote down the details of nearly every activity and speech in shorthand.

◼ ◼ ◼ "RETURN TO JUNGLE LAW"

The Defiance Campaign continued while its leaders were dealing with their court cases. By late September, more than 2,345 defiers were imprisoned and the jails in some areas, such as the eastern Cape region, were filled. The volunteers were refusing to post bail (a sum of money to guarantee that released prisoners would return for trial) and go home. That put the Malan government in an awkward position. The prime minister was forced to send the chief of police and warden of prisons to Port Elizabeth to negotiate with the ANC executive committee. Malan asked the group to temporarily halt the Defiance Campaign until all the prisoners could be processed and sent home. The point of the campaign was to fill the jails with defiers and cause the legal system to break down, so this was seen as a victory. As ANC activist William Nkomo declared at a Pretoria press conference, "Today we witness the turning point in the history of South Africa."

By early October, the Defiance Campaign was spreading to smaller towns in the eastern Cape region. Defiers were arrested, and workers held strikes in support of the volunteers. However, the ANC discovered that the feeling of rebellion sweeping through the townships could not be controlled by the well-organized structure of the Defiance Campaign. Trouble started in mid-October, when a white police officer accosted a black man getting off a train at the New Brighton station in Port Elizabeth. The man had allegedly stolen some cans of paint. A scuffle followed as police tried to arrest him. One of the police officers took out his gun and shot the suspect and another black man who was trying to help him. Other Africans in the station rushed to the scene and began throwing stones at the officers. They responded with gunfire, killing five in the crowd. The murders sparked a protest later in the day. An angry mob set fire to a movie theater, a post office, and several businesses. The white theater owner, his son, and two other bystanders were killed by rioters.

No ANC leaders were in New Brighton that day. However, the minister of native affairs, Hendrik Frensch Verwoerd, flew to Port Elizabeth the next day. Without investigating, he blamed the Youth League for inciting the riot. Ninety people were arrested in connection with the riots, including many ANC members.

After the New Brighten incident, authorities banned public gatherings and tightened curfews in Port Elizabeth. Hoping to cool tempers, the ANC leadership issued a statement on October 18, speaking out against violence while maintaining the righteousness of their cause:

> [The ANC] wishes to express the sincerest sympathy of the African people towards those families, both Black and White, who have suffered the loss of their loved ones through this unfortunate, reckless, ill-considered return to jungle law. This incident serves to bring to the notice of the public, forcibly, the danger of the doctrine of apartheid and race hatred, where differences between individuals immediately assume a racial character. . . . The A.N.C. calls upon the African people to cease forthwith from participating in any violent action. They must rally to the call of the A.N.C., which is conducting a non-violent struggle against racially discriminatory, unjust laws.

■ ■ ■ ■ A BADGE OF HONOR

Despite the ANC message, tension continued to escalate. In the first week of November, a riot broke out in Johannesburg. Five days later, another riot occurred in Kimberley. Twenty people were killed in the two incidents, leading the ANC to hold an open-air prayer service in the town of East London on November 9. While the service was taking place, the police arrived and declared that the gathering was a political meeting and therefore illegal. The ANC, however, had obtained permission from local authorities to hold a religious service. When police ordered the crowd to disperse, some began throwing stones at the officers. They responded by shooting their automatic rifles into the crowd. Another riot ensued. Angry black protesters killed two white bystanders including a nurse who was mutilated by her attackers.

After the riot, the government once again blamed the Defiance Campaign for the violence, a message widely promoted by the white-owned newspaper *Die Burger*: "For a while [during the riots] primitive Africa ruled, stripped of the varnish of civilization and free from the taming influence of the white man."

Hoping to change public perceptions, the ANC and the SAIC held a public meeting in Johannesburg. They wanted to explain that the campaign was trying to overturn unjust laws, not harm white people. However, only about two hundred whites attended. Most were members of the Communist Party or trade unions.

Members of the Black Sash movement demonstrate against apartheid outside the South African parliament in Cape Town in the 1950s. The Black Sash was a nonviolent white women's movement in South Africa opposed to apartheid.

In November 1952, when police fired on ANC members at a religious service, sparking a riot, the ANC National Action Committee issued the following statement. It accused the Malan administration of using police violence as a tool of systematic repression:

> These shootings are a part of the Government's plot to weaken the DEFIANCE CAMPAIGN and to ruthlessly oppress the non-European people.
>
> THE GOVERNMENT WANTS TO CREATE race riots between European and non-European, Indian and African, and African and Coloured; TO USE the riots and general disturbances to cause panic among the Europeans so as to drive them into the arms of the Nationalists; TO DECLARE a state of National Emergency, to seize absolute power, to cut off the leaders from the people and to impose a fascist dictatorship on the country.
>
> THEIR METHODS ARE TO SEND OUT agents among the people to provoke incidents which can be used by the police as a pretext for shooting and to incite and preach race hatred. . . .
>
> BEWARE! DO NOT be provoked—Do not listen to those who preach violence—Avoid rioting—Follow Congress' lead—BE PEACEFUL, DISCIPLINED, NON-VIOLENT. . . .
>
> LET US NOT ALLOW OURSELVES TO BE DIVERTED FROM THE COURSE OF ACTION LAID DOWN BY OUR CONGRESSES.

Despite efforts by the organizers, the riot significantly slowed the momentum of the Defiance Campaign. While the majority of volunteers supported the nonviolent goals of defiance, it was increasingly clear that any protests would be met with extreme force on the part of the authorities. Even Mandela later admitted that the campaign had carried on too long and it should have been halted at the height of its success in early September. Instead, it dragged on into December, ending with a few small protests scattered about the country.

The impact of the Defiance Campaign varied from place to place. About 70 percent of the defiance actions occurred in the eastern Cape region, with Port Elizabeth attracting most of the protests. This showed the campaign to be an urban movement, supported by middle-class African workers and educated, professional blacks. Still, many considered the Defiance Campaign a success despite its limited reach. By the time it ended, 8,057 people had been arrested. This was the largest example of mass disobedience ever carried out in South Africa. Mandela explains how the campaign helped the antiapartheid movement:

> The Defiance Campaign marked a new chapter in the struggle. . . . Prior to the campaign, the ANC was more talk than action. We had no paid organizers, no staff, and a membership that did little more than pay lip service to our cause. As a result of the campaign . . . the ANC emerged as a truly mass-based organization with an impressive corps of experienced activists who had braved the police, the courts, the jails. The stigma usually associated with imprisonment had been removed. This was a significant achievement, for fear of prison is a tremendous hindrance to a liberation struggle. From the Defiance Campaign onward, going to prison became a badge of honor among Africans.

■ ■ ■ HARSH NEW LAWS

On December 2, 1952, while the Defiance Campaign was grinding to a halt, Mandela and the other activists were back in court. Rumpff found all defendants guilty of statutory (legal) Communism. The magistrate pointed out that this was not Communism as it was practiced in the Soviet Union. Instead, as defined in the Suppression of Communism Act, it was a philosophy that attempted to bring about political or social change. The defiers were sentenced to nine months in prison with hard labor, but the sentence was suspended (put off) for three years. Although Rumpff was known as a tough magistrate, many saw this as a lenient sentence, since the activists could avoid jail by staying out of trouble. Rumpff explained why he did not immediately imprison the planners of the Defiance Campaign: "I accept the evidence that you have consistently advised your followers to follow a peaceful course of action and to avoid violence in any shape or form."

Even as the activists were praised by the judge for their commitment to nonviolence, the Malan administration was working to write harsh new laws to deal with public protests. In February 1953, Parliament enacted the Public Safety Act. This gave provincial governors power to proclaim a state of emergency during mass protests. Another statute, the Criminal Law Amendment Act, made it a crime to advise, encourage, incite, or command other people to protest against any law. The Criminal Law Amendment Act also took aim at low-ranking members who followed leaders of organizations such as the ANC and the SAIC. The act made it a crime to be in the company of anyone previously found guilty of protesting. Suspects were guilty unless they could prove their innocence. Those convicted of breaking the law could receive a prison term of three years, a fine of three hundred pounds (about ten thousand dollars), and a whipping.

A third new law was directed at protesters who tried to use white-only facilities. Prior to 1953, railways, restaurants, parks, and other facilities were required to provide separate accommodations for Europeans and nonwhites. However, the courts generally held the view that although the facilities were separate, they must be equal in quality. The Reservation of Separate Amenities Act erased the concept of separate but equal. The new law held that separate amenities for nonwhites need not be provided. If separate facilities were available, they need not be of good or even usable quality. This essentially gave permission to owners of hotels, theaters, restaurants, and shops to exclude nonwhites by not providing separate amenities. The Reservation of Separate Amenities Act also specified that it was a crime for persons of one race to use the facilities set aside for another.

Another change dealt with protesters who thought it was a badge of honor to serve short prison sentences for violating apartheid laws. To stem the tide of arrests, the ministry of justice enacted a regulation meant to deter defiers. Nonwhites sentenced to six months or less could be sent to prisons built by farmers in rural areas. Farmers could force the prisoners to work in the fields. The minister of justice, C. R. Swart, said this plan was meant to keep minor offenders out of the jail system, where they would be exposed to hardened criminals. But the farm prison system used prisoners as slave laborers. Abuse of the system was rampant in Transvaal, where men were arrested and sent to work on

Armed guards march prisoners to a field to work as part of South Africa's farm prison system in the 1950s.

farms even before they were convicted of a crime. Court cases also documented that prisoners were beaten and starved and several died in captivity.

"A WHITE MAN'S COUNTRY"

The Defiance Campaign was over. While it helped rally thousands to the antiapartheid cause, it also ultimately strengthened the Nationalist government. In the 1953 general election, Malan easily won reelection by running a campaign based on fear of the "black danger." The NP significantly increased its majority in Parliament. The Nationalists

"Either the White man dominates or the Black man takes over. . . . The only way the Europeans can maintain supremacy is by domination. . . . And the only way they can maintain domination is by withholding the vote from the Non-Europeans. . . . It is because the voting power is in the hands of the White man that the White man is able to govern South Africa today. Under the existing law it is not possible for the Natives, through merit or any other means, to get the government into their hands. . . . To suggest that the White man can maintain leadership purely on the grounds of his greater competency is unrealistic. The greater competency of the White man can never weigh against numbers if Natives and Europeans enjoy equal voting rights."

—Johannes Strydom, South African prime minister, 1954

Afrikaners enjoy a sunny day at the beach in Cape Town in 1953. The white minority in South Africa enjoyed a much higher standard of living than the country's black majority.

regarded their victory as proof that the people supported apartheid.

Malan retired at the age of eighty in 1954. By this time, his vision of repressive apartheid was firmly entrenched in South African society. Johannes Strydom (also spelled Strijdom) was named prime minister. He was the former leader of an extreme right-wing group of Transvaal Nationalists who were even more uncompromising on matters of race than Malan. When Strydom took control of South Africa's government on November 30, he announced, "The Europeans must stand their ground and remain Baas [boss] in South Africa.... [In] every sphere the Europeans must retain the right to rule the country and to keep it a white man's country."

Strydom's views were supported by an overwhelming majority of Afrikaners. His words were backed by an authoritarian national security apparatus (police force) skilled at ferociously repressing any resistance to apartheid. Meanwhile, members of the ANC, the SAIC, and other antiapartheid groups were restricted by permits, curfews, bannings, and dozens of petty laws that they seemed helpless to resist. It seemed the campaign based on Gandhian nonviolence had not ended apartheid but strengthened it instead.

CHAPTER 5

VIOLENT
RESISTANCE

"The people's patience is not endless. The time comes in the life of any nation when there remain only two choices—submit or fight. That time has now come to South Africa."

—Umkhonto we Sizwe (Spear of the Nation, a revolutionary organization), statement, December 16, 1961

In April 1953, the South African Nationalist government returned for a second term in office and continued to tighten its grip on power with a barrage of new laws. The Bantu Education Act of 1953 brought mission schools under government control. These schools were the only places that black children could receive a quality education. But with the new law in place, mission schools had to teach government-approved topics and implement rigid rules of conduct for teachers and students. Native affairs minister Verwoerd explained why the government wanted to restrict educational opportunities: "There is no place for [the Bantu] in the European community above the level of certain forms of labour. What is the use of teaching the Bantu child mathematics when

In protest of the Bantu Education Act of 1953, many black African parents and children boycotted government-run schools.

it cannot be used in practice? That is quite absurd." Despite Verwoerd's mention of math, the Bantu Education Act was intended to destroy the mission education system that produced such activists as Nelson Mandela and Oliver Tambo.

In addition to passing new restrictions, the government obsessively enforced the old rules. Annually more than three hundred thousand people, or one in ten black citizens, were convicted of violating the pass laws that restricted the movements of nonwhites. Prosecutions under the Immorality Act, which forbade sexual relations between people of different races, also continued at a high rate. A small army of morality police enforced the law by hiding in trees and peering into windows to catch mixed-race couples engaged in lovemaking. A more harmful law, the Urban Areas Act, was strictly enforced so that a servant could only live in a white area if employed there. This meant that married people could not live with their spouses and children if they worked and lived on land owned by whites.

As the Nationalists fanatically enforced apartheid, resistance to the system weakened. Hundreds of black leaders were banned from public life. Some were exiled to distant reserves in rural areas, forcing them to give up their careers, homes, and families. In 1954 leading ANC organizer Robert Resha described how government restrictions had slowed the liberation movement:

> The old methods of bringing about mass action through public mass meetings, press statements, and leaflets calling upon the people to go into action have become extremely dangerous and difficult to use effectively. The authorities will not easily permit a meeting under the auspices of the ANC; few newspapers will publish statements openly criticizing the policies of the government; and there is hardly a single printing press which will agree to print leaflets calling up workers to embark upon industrial action. . . . These developments require the evolution of new forms of political struggle which will make it possible for us to strive for action on a higher level than the defiance campaign.

Left: **Robert Resha was a Youth League president and organizer in the 1950s.**
Right: **Zachariah Matthews, a professor at the University of Fort Hare, envisioned a Congress of the People.**

THE FREEDOM CHARTER

The new plan of action envisioned by Resha was based on an idea that originated with Zachariah Matthews, a professor at Fort Hare. Matthews had a vision of forming a Congress of the People, which would represent Africans, Indians, mixed race, and whites who believed in banishing apartheid and replacing it with democracy.

On June 25, 1955, Matthews's dream of the Congress of the People became reality. Three thousand delegates defied apartheid restrictions and police intimidation to meet in an open field in Kliptown, near Johannesburg. Attendees represented the ANC, the SAIC, the Coloured Peoples Organization, and a white organization called the Congress of Democrats. The hall was surrounded by police officers as delegates inside wrote a constitution called the

The Congress of the People heard the Freedom Charter read aloud on June 26, 1955, at Kliptown before police broke up the gathering.

Freedom Charter. The document pointed out that the Nationalist government was antidemocratic and based on promoting injustice and inequality. It asserted "South Africa belongs to all who live in it" and "all shall be equal before the law."

Language in the charter held that people would only be prosperous and free when they were treated equally regardless of their color, race, sex, or beliefs. It called for a sharing of mining wealth, land redistribution, fair trials, free speech, the right to form unions, and the right of the people to live and travel freely. The Freedom Charter concluded with these words, emphasized in capital letters: "THESE FREEDOMS WE WILL FIGHT FOR, SIDE BY SIDE, THROUGHOUT OUR LIVES, UNTIL WE HAVE WON OUR LIBERTY."

On June 26, 1955, the Congress of the People adopted the Freedom Charter. The main points of the 1,265-word document follow:

> We, the people of South Africa, declare for all our country and the world to know: that South Africa belongs to all who live in it, black and white, and that no government can justly claim authority unless it is based on the will of the People; that our people have been robbed of their birthright to land, liberty and peace by a form of government founded on injustice and inequality; that our country will never be prosperous or free until all our people live in brotherhood, enjoying equal rights and opportunities; that only a democratic state, based on the will of all the people, can secure to all their birthright without distinction of colour, race, sex or belief.

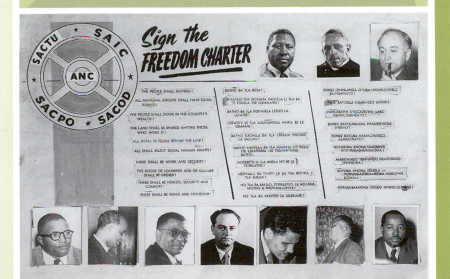

Among the authors of the Freedom Charter were Albert Luthuli _(upper left)_ and Walter Sisulu _(third from lower left)._

On June 26, heavily armed police shut down the Congress of the People. However, before the delegates left, they read the Freedom Charter in full. The document was the first formulated by South Africans to express their unique vision of an alternative society. The Strydom government viewed the words as treasonous. On September 27, three months after the conclusion of the Congress of the People, more than one thousand members of the Special Branch police force launched the biggest raid in South African history. They searched hundreds of homes and seized diaries, papers, letters, and notebooks. More than five hundred people were held under the Suppression of Communism Act. Sporadic raids continued for another year as investigators compiled evidence for a mass trial.

On December 5, 1956, the investigation ended with the arrest of 156 high-level activists, including doctors, lawyers, teachers, journalists, and several white liberal politicians. Leaders caught in the raid included Matthews, Mandela, Sisulu, Tambo, and Dadoo. All were indicted (charged) with high treason. The words in the Freedom Charter served as the basis for the indictment. If convicted, defendants could receive the death penalty.

Special Branch detectives search through the files of the Natal Indian Congress in 1955 to find evidence of Communist activity.

Although the 156 black, mixed-race, Indian, and white defendants ranged from political moderates to Communist revolutionaries, they faced trial as a group. The spectacle was held in a large military hall. For the first few days, the defendants were forced to sit in a cage of wire-mesh netting 6 feet (1.8 m) high. (The cage was eventually removed.) The preliminary examinations went on for months as ten thousand documents were entered into court records and dozens of detectives were called to testify. In September 1957, the trial was adjourned (ended). The attorney general dropped charges against all but twenty-nine defendants. The treason trial for these twenty-nine dragged on for several more years. Suddenly, in March 1961, those who remained, including Mandela, were found not guilty by three judges of the South African Supreme Court. After the longest and largest trial in South Africa history, the judges

From left: **Robert Resha, Patrick Molaoa, and Nelson Mandela arrive in Johannesburg in 1958 for their trial.**

decided that ANC was not a Communist organization and its members did not promote violent revolution. No one was convicted. But the trial attracted a great deal of negative press in Great Britain, the United States, and elsewhere. During the years it dragged on, sympathetic activists in Western democracies raised 173,000 pounds (about $4.5 million) to help the defendants fight the charges.

■ ■ ■ CREATING BANTUSTANS

By the time the treason trial ended, a new level of rage was driving the antiapartheid movement. In 1958 Prime Minister Strydom died and was replaced by Hendrik Verwoerd. Whites and blacks alike were afraid of the new prime minister. The opposition United Party depicted Verwoerd as unstable, a man "crazed by his dream of complete territorial segregation of the races."

One of Verwoerd's first acts sought to remove black people completely from South Africa's social, cultural, and political affairs. To achieve this goal, he proposed that Parliament pass the Promotion of Bantu Self-Government Bill of 1959. This law dealt with the 250 scattered reserves created by the Native Lands Act in 1913. The Promotion of Bantu Self-Government Bill combined the reserves into eight large Bantu homelands, called Bantustans. These regions, much like Native American reservations in the United States, were to be considered independent nations.

Bantustans were governed by black chiefs and headmen, who were paid by the apartheid government. Local administrators formed semi-independent governments that could tax Bantustan residents, control public lands, and hold local trials. This bill transferred the burden of social welfare costs and unemployment responsibilities to the Bantustans. It forced homelands to come up with ways to become self-sufficient by building their own economies. However, the Bantustans had no natural resources or industries and very primitive electric, sewer, and telephone systems. Black Africans who had jobs did not have to live on the Bantustans. They would be permitted to reside with their white employers, although families would be forced to move to the reserves.

However, workers who did not perform adequately or who took part in protests could be fired and forced to relocate to the poverty-stricken Bantustans. The bill was a blatant attempt to exert government control over Africans. As the minister of Bantu administration, Michiel C. Botha, stated: "Natives without work or who, as approved workers, misbehaved, [will] disappear out of white South Africa, back to the reserves."

By creating Bantustans, Verwoerd did away with government responsibility for South Africa's black citizens without providing resources for them to sustain their communities. The worst part of the Promotion of Bantu Self-Government Bill was that it deprived blacks of their South African citizenship. As the Verwoerd administration saw it, residents of Bantustans were no longer South Africa's problem because they were not citizens of that nation.

■ ■ ■ THE SHARPEVILLE MASSACRE

Resistance to the Promotion of Bantu Self-Government Bill was fierce. Another controversial issue concerned the government's decision to require black women who worked off the reserves to carry passes. Black men had been subject to pass laws for decades. Each black male was required to carry a pass book that listed his name, birthplace, and tribe. The pass contained a photo, a serial number, and a space to list arrests. Unless it was signed by his employer each month, the pass holder could be forced to move to a Bantustan, where there were thousands of other unemployed people.

On March 21, 1960, the Pan Africanist Congress (PAC) organized a protest against the hated pass laws in the black township of Sharpeville, 28 miles (45 km) southwest of Johannesburg. Although the PAC was a rival group to the ANC, the act of civil disobedience was modeled on the Defiance Campaign. About six thousand people went to the Sharpeville police station without passes and asked to be arrested. After a long standoff, authorities grew nervous, fearing that the crowd was about to storm the station. Police opened fire without warning on the unarmed, peaceful crowd killing 69 protesters and wounding 186. Many were shot in the back as they tried to escape the gunfire.

Top: A crowd gathers in Sharpeville to protest pass laws.
Bottom: Nervous police officers shot into the Sharpeville crowd, killing sixty-eight people. The massacre outraged people around the world.

Reaction to the Sharpeville Massacre was immediate and widespread. The PAC and the ANC organized strikes and demonstrations. The anger spiraled out of control, resulting in violent riots. The government reacted by declaring a state of emergency and rounding up eighteen hundred people who organized or participated in the uprisings.

The massacre and the government's reaction brought unwanted international attention. On April 1, apartheid was condemned at the United Nations. This international peacekeeping organization passed Resolution 134, calling on South Africa to institute democratic reforms to guarantee equality to all of its citizens.

■ ■ ■ LAUNCHING AN ARMED STRUGGLE

The Sharpeville Massacre was not the first time large numbers of protesters had been murdered by police. But the event marked a new phase in South Africa's long struggle. The voices of those who were preaching nonviolent resistance were drowned out by people advocating armed rebellion. Even Mandela could no long justify passive resistance. As he later explained, it was "only when all else had failed, when all channels of peaceful progress had been barred to us, that the decision was made to embark on violent forms of political struggle. . . . The Government had left us with no choice."

South Africa's violent revolutionary struggle began during what was called the Year of Africa. In 1960 thirteen African nations gained independence from France, Great Britain, and Belgium. In 1961 Tambo commented on these developments: "This is Africa's age—the dawn of her fulfillment. Yes, the moment when she must grapple with destiny to reach the summit saying—ours was a fight for noble values and worthy ends, and not for lands and the enslavement of men. To us all, free and not free, the call of the hour is to redeem the name and honor of Mother Africa."

To redeem Africa's honor, military groups formed in the PAC and the ANC. These two groups outwardly maintained their dedication to nonviolence. On December 11, 1961, members of the PAC founded a military group called Poqo, meaning "only" or "pure." Five days later,

In the 1950s and 1960s, powerful European nations decolonized the African countries they had been governing for centuries. The United Nations declared 1960 the Year of Africa when France granted independence to present-day Togo, Mali, Senegal, Madagascar, Benin, Niger, Burkina Faso, Côte d'Ivoire (Ivory Coast), Chad, the Central African Republic, Congo, Gabon, and Mauritania. That year Somalia, Cameroon, and Nigeria achieved independence from Great Britain. Belgium pulled its government administrators out of the Democratic Republic of the Congo in 1960 and Rwanda and Burundi in 1962. Then other African nations achieved independence in the years that followed, including Algeria, Sierra Leone, Uganda, Kenya, Malawi, Zambia, Gambia, Botswana, and Lesotho. The independence movement made it much more difficult for South African leaders to justify their repressive apartheid policies in the face of a widespread democratic revolution sweeping the African continent.

Mandela helped found the Umkhonto we Sizwe (MK), or "Spear of the Nation." Members came from the ANC and Communist Party. At its first meeting, the high command of Umkhonto we Sizwe issued a statement:

> The time comes in the life of any nation when there remain only two choices: submit or fight. That time has now come to South Africa. We shall not submit and we have no choice but to hit back by all means within our power in defense of our people, our future and our freedom.

Membership within the MK was open to all races. The group identified four options it intended to pursue—sabotage, guerrilla warfare, terrorism, and open revolution. In its first several years, MK militants attacked power stations and government buildings including pass offices, native courts, and post offices. While the group intended to destroy buildings that represented apartheid, actions were always conducted in the early morning hours to ensure no innocent civilians were injured or killed.

Government officials investigate the destruction of power lines in the 1960s. It was an act of sabotage by the MK.

■ ■ ■ "I AM PREPARED TO DIE"

At the time Mandela helped found the MK, he was banned from organizing by a court order. This required him to go underground (disappear from public view.) Beginning in 1961, Mandela lived in secret locations such as empty apartments. He slept during the day and worked at night. When he went out in public, he disguised himself as a chef, a chauffeur, or a gardener in blue overalls. By this time, Mandela was divorced from his first wife and married to Winnie Madikizela-Mandela. They had been together for three years, yet the couple could only meet in secret on rare occasions. Most of the time, Winnie had to read rumors in the *Rand Daily Mail* to find out where her husband had been spotted.

Mandela was able to elude police for seventeen months. But on August 5, 1962, the U.S. Central Intelligence Agency (CIA), which supported the South African battle against Communism, tipped off authorities as to his whereabouts. Mandela was arrested. Two days later, he was charged with inciting worker strikes the previous year. On October 25, 1962, the leader of the ANC was sentenced to five years of hard labor. The government believed Mandela had committed other crimes while directing the MK. In July 1963, agents arrested the entire high command of the organization, including Sisulu. These men, along with Mandela, were put on trial for sabotage and crimes

Nelson Mandela speaks at a conference in 1961. Three years later, he was sentenced to prison for life.

relating to treason. Mandela and eight others were sent to prison for life on June 12, 1964. In his last statement before the court, the forty-five-year-old Mandela said:

> During my lifetime I have dedicated myself to this struggle of the African people. I have fought against white domination, and I have fought against black domination. I have cherished the ideal of a democratic and free society in which all persons live together in harmony and with equal opportunities. It is an ideal which I hope to live for and to achieve. But if needs be, it is an ideal for which I am prepared to die.

Mandela served most of his sentence on Robben Island, in Table Bay, about 4 miles (6.4 km) off the coast of Cape Town.

■ ■ ■ ■ DETAINED WITHOUT CHARGES

With many leading activists in jail, two powerful government officials came up with a plan to crush opposition to apartheid. Minister of Justice John Vorster and Bureau of State Security (BOSS) general Hendrik J. van den Bergh were both outspoken supporters of the Nazis during World War II. The men were authors of the new security legislation. Called the General Law Amendment of 1963, it allowed police to arrest any South African citizen and hold him or her for ninety days without filing charges or providing access to a lawyer. After that time, police could immediately rearrest and hold the person for another ninety days. No South African court could order the person's release. Only the minister of justice had that power.

By denying judges and lawyers any role concerning detainees (prisoners), South Africa moved one step closer to a totalitarian state. In such a state, the central government exerts complete control over the political activities of the people. The new law received international condemnation. Yet it helped make Vorster one of the most popular politicians in South Africa. In 1966 Verwoerd was assassinated by a parliamentary messenger angered by the Prohibition of Mixed

Marriages Act. This law prevented him from marrying his mixed-race girlfriend. After Verwoerd's death, Vorster was elected prime minister.

By this time, the MK was concentrating on building an army outside South Africa. Hundreds of members trained in Algeria, Tanzania, and the Soviet Union. Meanwhile, Poqo soldiers were being trained by guerrilla war experts in the People's Republic of China.

Despite their continued training, the militias were limited by geography. They needed friendly countries from which to operate. But the nations surrounding South Africa were friendly to the apartheid regime. The military groups were unable to cross borders to fight in South Africa. With low morale, desertion within the ranks was widespread.

■ ■ ■ SHOCKING RESETTLEMENT OPERATIONS

In 1967, with little internal opposition, Vorster stepped up a program to force all black South Africans to relocate to Bantustans. The reserves were populated with more people than they could feed. Yet several million Africans living in areas claimed by whites were forced to sell their livestock and move. Despite the obvious hardship the relocations were causing the victims, the minister of Bantu administration, M. C. Botha, boldly stated: "The Bantu people like being moved. . . . They like the places where they are being resettled."

Resettlement operations were carried out by soldiers who loaded hundreds of people into cattle trucks. Most of the relocations were carried out in secret, at night, so that average citizens were unaware of what was happening. However, in 1970, a British television crew filmed a documentary called *The Dumping Grounds*. It exposed the crimes against humanity committed by the Vorster administration.

Filmmakers focused on a township near Kimberley that had been set aside for Africans in the 1930s. This township was in the middle of a European area. Seven thousand Africans were loaded onto trucks and taken hundreds of miles away to a Bantu reserve called Kuruman on the edge of the Kalahari Desert. The blacks were abandoned on land that was totally unsuitable for growing crops or raising livestock.

Within weeks, hundreds were starving and more than two hundred died. When the camera crew returned two years later, starvation was rampant. As a local doctor commented, "The incidence of malnutrition here is shocking, even to someone accustomed to African conditions."

THE BLACK CONSCIOUSNESS MOVEMENT

The policies of the Vorster administration succeeded in stifling protest and revolutionary activities. However, one aspect of the apartheid educational policy of the 1950s had unintended consequences that began to affect the country in the early 1970s. In 1957 Prime Minister Verwoerd instituted the Extension of University Education Act, which enforced strict segregation in institutions of higher learning. The majority of the country's universities were already restricted to whites. Fort Hare, at-

Steve Biko

tended by many leaders of the ANC, was all-black. However, three mostly white universities had a total of 1,225 nonwhite students, who were taught in segregated classrooms. Verwoerd wanted to expel all black students from white colleges. This move turned out to be extremely unpopular with university professors. To please the teachers, the government decided to build several new, all-black universities, called tribal colleges.

By the late 1960s, activists at tribal colleges were filling the leadership vacuum left by the imprisoned founders of the ANC and MK. A charismatic young medical student named Steve Biko was the leader of the new generation.

Medical student Steve Biko founded the South African Students' Organisation in 1969. It became the Black Consciousness Movement (BCM), which worked to foster racial pride in black South Africans. Biko had this to say about the Black Consciousness Movement in 1978:

> Black Consciousness is an attitude of mind and a way of life, the most positive call to emanate [come] from the black world for a long time. Its essence is the realization by the black man of the need to rally together with his brothers around the cause of their oppression—the blackness of their skin—and to operate as a group to rid themselves of the shackles that bind them to perpetual servitude. It is based on a self-examination, which has ultimately led them to believe that by seeking to run away from themselves and emulate [imitate] the white man, they are insulting the intelligence of whoever created them black. . . .

> At the heart of this kind of thinking is the realization by blacks that the most potent weapon in the hands of the oppressor is the mind of the oppressed. If one is free at heart, no man-made chains can bind one to servitude, but if one's mind is so manipulated and controlled by the oppressor as to make the oppressed believe that he is a liability to the white man, then there will be nothing the oppressed can do to scare his powerful masters. Hence thinking along lines of Black Consciousness makes the black man see himself as a being complete in himself. It makes him less dependent and more free to express his manhood. At the end of it all he cannot tolerate attempts by anybody to dwarf the significance of his manhood.

Biko founded the all-black South African Students' Organisation (SASO) in 1969. SASO based its philosophy on the Pan-African ideals of black self-reliance and the concept of Africa for Africans.

In the early 1970s, SASO transformed itself into the Black Consciousness Movement. This racial pride movement supported free speech and resistance to apartheid. Despite its name, the Black Consciousness Movement was open to all people of color and included many Indians. The most unique aspect of the BCM was its focus on black feelings of racial inferiority. Like many nonwhites in South Africa, Biko was raised to believe that white culture was superior. Over the centuries, this belief created a sense of inferiority in black people. It prevented them from improving their situation. As Biko wrote:

> Black Consciousness seeks to channel the pent-up forces of the angry black masses to meaningful and directional opposition. . . . But the type of black man we have today has lost his manhood. Reduced to an obliging shell, he looks with awe at the white power structure and accepts what he regards as the 'inevitable position.' . . . The black man has become a shadow, completely defeated, drowning in his own misery, a slave and ox bearing the yoke of oppression with sheepish timidity.

Biko's words resonated with a large number of nonwhite South Africans. The BCM message was spread through groups called Formation Schools that provided leadership seminars to students and nonstudents alike. The young leaders trained in the Formation Schools helped establish self-help groups to deal with feelings of black inferiority. The BCM also published several journals to broadcast its message, including *Black Review, Black Voice, Black Perspective,* and *Creativity in Development.*

The main goal of the BCM was to create a black South Africa where whites would live by the rules made by nonwhites. The government believed this message led to revolution and instituted a new measure to control students. In 1975 the minister of Bantu education issued an order that arithmetic and social study classes in Bantu secondary schools would be taught in Afrikaans, not the traditional English. Teachers, parents, and students were outraged. In multilingual South Africa, business and commerce was conducted in English. Afrikaans was the language used by Nationalist politicians, police, and prison wardens.

Objections to the language policy erupted into violence. On June 16, 1976, fifteen thousand students held a mass rally at a secondary school in the township of Soweto, 10 miles (16 km) from Johannesburg. Speakers, using the language of the Black Consciousness Movement, explained that Afrikaans was the language of the oppressors. Since most students spoke English, the use of this language for lessons would create feelings of inferiority in students.

Students in Soweto take to the streets to protest the forced use of Afrikaans in school lessons in 1976.

The peaceful rally, filled with schoolchildren, was suddenly interrupted by police who arrived to break up the crowd. Officers fired tear gas and then opened fire, killing two and wounding countless others. Thousands who escaped went on a rampage through Soweto, throwing stones, turning over cars, and setting fire to shops and government buildings. Two white officials were murdered. In the days that followed, the anger spread to townships throughout the country. For weeks, riots, fires, and explosions occurred around school buildings. Police retaliated with bullwhips, batons, and bullets. In Johannesburg four strikes between August and November 1976 brought the city to a halt. The violence continued for an entire year during which at least 575 people were killed and 2,398 were wounded.

Police rounded up political activists, hoping to quell the uprising. In 1976 the twenty-nine-year-old Biko was arrested and held under the Terrorism Act for 101 days without charge. He was arrested again on August 18, 1977. By this time, Biko was an internationally respected figure. He had held meetings with newspaper editors, journalists, diplomats, and U.S. senators to discuss the situation in South Africa. His status did little to help him with the police, however. On September 7, after being manacled (handcuffed) and naked for twenty days, Biko was taken to an interrogation room and severely beaten. He died of massive head injuries on September 12. Police falsely listed his cause of death as a hunger strike.

The Vorster administration had underestimated Biko's popularity. His death was widely condemned in democratic countries throughout the world. Biko's funeral was attended by more than fifteen thousand people, including ambassadors and diplomats from the United States and twelve other Western democracies.

PRESSURE FROM WITHIN AND WITHOUT

By the time of Biko's death, the international community was beginning to unite in its opposition to apartheid. Jimmy Carter was elected president of the United States in 1976. He strongly opposed South

More than fifteen thousand people attended the funeral of Steve Biko, the founder of South Africa's Black Consciousness Movement.

African Nationalist policies. Carter's vice president, Walter Mondale, told Vorster that the United States supported the ANC's call for universal voting rights in South Africa. Antiapartheid sentiments also grew in Britain and in other parts of Europe, based on a UN resolution passed in 1973 that declared apartheid a crime against humanity. To isolate the Vorster government, the UN instituted a mandatory arms and oil embargo (trade restrictions) against South Africa in 1977.

The worldwide condemnation resulted in an economic disaster as investors and businesses fled South Africa. Meanwhile, thousands of students energized by the BCM and hardened by the Soweto riots fled across South Africa's northern border. The activists went to Mozambique and Angola, which had achieved independence in 1974 and 1975, respectively. There, they served as volunteers in the small guerrilla forces maintained by the ANC and the PAC. Known as the June 16th Detachment, after the first day of the Soweto riot, their numbers and their experiences led to a new phase in the armed struggle against apartheid.

In the MK, members of the June 16th Detachment received basic training and specialized courses in communications, intelligence, engineering, and artillery training. Recruits sneaked back into South Africa, where they helped build the ANC underground movement. They carried out acts of sabotage against police stations, railway lines, and government institutions. One attack in June 1980 against the Sasol Oil refinery complex caused sixty-six million pounds ($336 million) in damages.

By this time, South Africa had a new prime minister, Pieter W. Botha. Elected in 1978, Botha was a longtime leader of the Nationalist Party. He was considered less reactionary (opposed to social change) than his predecessor. Botha, like many other South Africans, was beginning to see that apartheid in its current form was not sustainable. The new generation of militant activists would never return to the days of passive defiance. Two decades of chaos and police violence proved that one side in the battle over South Africa's future was never going to back down.

CHAPTER 6

THE END
OF
APARTHEID

"The new era which is dawning in our country, beneath the great southern stars, will lift us out of the silent grief of our past and into a future in which there will be opportunity and space for joy and beauty—for real and lasting peace."

—South African president F. W. de Klerk, Nobel lecture, 1993

By the late 1970s, South Africa's apartheid government was facing international condemnation and violent opposition at home. While the new prime minister, P. W. Botha, was as conservative as his predecessors, he was also pragmatic. He understood that apartheid could not survive in the long run. But Botha's desire to loosen the bonds of repression was based more on profits than politics. After the bloodshed of the 1976 Soweto riots, church leaders, liberal groups, and progressive investment firms began pressuring international companies to stop doing business in South Africa. Many multinational corporations closed their offices in the country.

White South Africans also had to deal with changing numbers that had nothing to do with the economy. The percentage of whites living in South Africa was steadily decreasing. In 1936 white people made up 21 percent of South Africa's population. By 1980 they were only 16 percent. A study in the late seventies projected that by 2000, the white population would only be 10 percent, while blacks would make up 83 percent of the total South African population.

Facing the inevitable, the Botha government moved toward a series of reforms. He said South Africa had to "adapt or die." The country was facing a choice between two situations, "the path of confrontation, bloodshed, nameless suffering, and the downfall of white civilization . . . or that of consultation and joint decision making with due regard for [racial] self-determination."

CONCESSIONS LARGE AND SMALL

The Botha administration did two studies to guide its reform programs. The Commission of Inquiry into Labour Legislation, or the Wiehahn Commission, concluded that strikes would be less common and less violent if black workers were allowed to form unions. This would give Africans a stake in the financial success of companies they worked for. The commission concluded that when earnings increased, the rising wealth of middle-class Africans would provide a stabilizing influence in South African society.

This new middle class would also provide a buffer between white society and the radicals in the ANC, the MK, the Poqo, the PAC, and the Communist Party. The commission recommendations led to the Labour Relations Act of 1981. Soon after, African trade unions experienced massive growth.

A second government study recommended that Botha eliminate what was known as "petty apartheid," the racial separation at public facilities bearing "Europeans Only" signs. Botha and many South African businesspeople supported the commission recommendations. By 1980 petty apartheid was no longer strictly enforced in Cape Town's hotels, restaurants, and theaters or on its bus service and beaches. However, petty apartheid remained in many other areas. Even in Cape Town, residential and school segregation remained throughout the 1980s.

The Botha government also set up a series of programs that would have been unthinkable in previous decades. Businesses received large tax breaks to train black workers for skilled industrial jobs. Africans

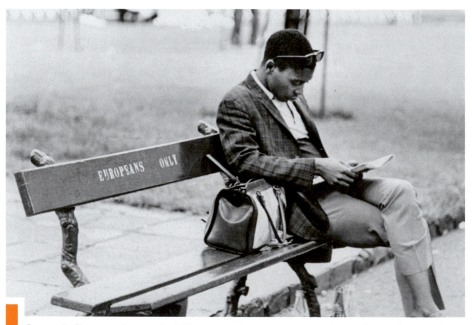

Open defiance of apartheid became more common throughout the 1970s. By 1980 most petty apartheid laws were no longer enforced in Cape Town.

could purchase property or obtain ninety-nine-year leases on land in townships.

THE UNITED DEMOCRATIC FRONT

Botha's most controversial move was the proposal of a new South African constitution in 1983. The constitution would eliminate the single house of Parliament and replace it with three governing bodies: a 178-member all-white House of Assembly, an 85-member mixed-race House of Representatives, and a 45-member Indian House of Delegates. The new constitution would abolish the post of prime minister and replace it with a state president. This person would be chosen by an electoral college in which white politicians were a permanent majority.

Africans, who made up 75 percent of the population, were not given any political power. This resulted in widespread criticism of the constitutional proposal. Botha answered the critics by explaining that Africans were not really citizens of South Africa since most resided on Bantustans. The government considered these to be separate states. Elections were held on Bantustans. Africans could vote for those who represented their interests within the townships.

Opposition to the new constitution was widespread, and a new political party united to oppose it. In August 1983, ten thousand delegates of all races met near Cape Town to form the United Democratic Front (UDF). Members of the UDF represented about four hundred organizations including student, church, and civic groups and even sports teams. But trade unions were the main force behind the UDF. They were now legal and their members could not be banned for political activities.

The UDF was dedicated to nonviolence. Its goal was to convince the government to do away with the constitutional reforms, abandon apartheid, and incorporate the homelands back into South Africa. Within months, the UDF grew to include three million individuals and six hundred organizations. The most outspoken activists in the group were two of South Africa's most revered religious leaders: Bishop Desmond Tutu and the Reverend Allan Boesak.

■ ■ ■ ■ MORE TROUBLES IN SHARPEVILLE

Despite the opposition, the new constitution went into effect on September 3, 1984. That same day, violence in Sharpeville made headlines around the world once again. This time, the bloodshed was not the fault of the police. It was a result of the voting rights in the new constitution.

In the September election, only 30 percent of registered mixed-race voters and only 20 percent of registered Indian voters cast ballots. But in black townships, where candidates were elected to represent local governments, the UDF had organized an election boycott. Only 3 percent of registered voters cast ballots. Most of the candidates for township mayoral and council posts were middle-class blacks who wanted to work with the white government to help the townships regain political legitimacy in South Africa.

In Sharpeville the anger against the Botha government erupted into violence on election day. The newly elected black deputy mayor was hacked to death by a machete-wielding mob. The crowd went on a rampage, burning and strangling twenty-six Africans and setting fire to

Violence erupted in Sharpeville again in September 1984 in response to race-based government policies.

stores and businesses. Similar events took place in the nearby township of Sebokeng.

The bloody rampage marked a turning point in South Africa. It was the first time black people killed other blacks for their perceived association with the apartheid government. In the five months that followed, black-on-black violence spread to nearly every township. According to government reports, at least 9 people were killed and 160 were injured. Among them were black councilors and police officers. In addition, nine black clinics, 143 schools, and six churches were destroyed along with 516 private vehicles and 1,080 buses. The violence also caused 147 fearful black politicians to resign their elected posts.

Images of the carnage were broadcast around the world. They did little to aid the antiapartheid cause. The Botha government used the images to support its argument that Africans were not ready for self-government.

■ ■ ■ NECKLACING

Ironically, the anarchy in the townships was taking place at a time when Desmond Tutu had become an international celebrity after winning the Nobel Peace Prize in October 1984. But by the end of that year, the South African government reported that 175 people were killed in political violence. And the situation continued to deteriorate. In July 1985, a young girl who was suspected of being a police informer was stoned, stabbed, and beaten at the funeral of a black police officer. Her body was covered with sticks and set on fire. Once again, the images of the violence were used by supporters of apartheid to portray black Africans negatively.

More acts of brutality were carried out by groups of young men called the comrades. These revolutionaries believed that any blacks in authority, whether police officers, councilors, or homeland leaders, were enemies. Their preferred method for dealing with enemies, called necklacing, horrified the world. A victim's hands would be chopped off or held by barbed wire. Then an old tire was placed around the victim's neck, filled with gasoline, and set on fire. The resulting blaze

Archbishop Desmond Tutu won the Nobel Peace Prize in 1984 (*opposite page, left*) for his efforts to end apartheid and promote social justice. During his acceptance speech, he gave examples of the tragedies that were part of daily life in South Africa:

> We visited the home of an old lady. She told us that she looked after her grandson and the children of neighbors while their parents were at work. One day the police chased some pupils who had been boycotting classes, but they disappeared between the township houses. The police drove down the old lady's street. She was sitting at the back of the house in her kitchen, whilst her charges were playing in the front of the house in the yard. Her daughter rushed into the house, calling out to her to come quickly. The old lady dashed out of the kitchen into the living room. Her grandson had fallen just inside the door, dead. He had been shot in the back by the police. He was six years old. A few

took about twenty minutes to kill the victim. Passersby were unable to help because the tire dripped a scorching tarlike substance that made the necklace impossible to remove.

Police patrols refused to enter some areas. This allowed the comrades to take control. Some comrades built parks and playgrounds and attempted to raise money to fix schools. Others set up mock courtrooms and doled out street justice to enemies with whips, batons, and necklaces. In 1985 the government issued a conservative estimate of eight hundred people killed in the violence that turned the townships into battlefields.

weeks later, a white mother, trying to register her black servant for work, drove through a black township. Black rioters stoned her car and killed her baby of a few months old, the first white casualty of the current unrest in South Africa. Such deaths are two too many. These are part of the high cost of apartheid.

The government took advantage of the situation and encouraged the carnage in several ways. As the white undercover police detective Eugene de Kock wrote in 1988:

> The black on black violence . . . was a handy propaganda tool because the outside world could be told . . . that the barbaric natives . . . started murdering each other at every opportunity. We contributed to this violence for a number of years both passively (by failing to take steps) and actively (by sponsoring training and protecting violent gangs).

■ ■ ■ BOTHA REACHES OUT TO MANDELA

Some of the gangs causing township violence were linked to a new antiapartheid group. It was formed by hundreds of supporters of the Black Consciousness Movement. They had recently been released from prison after being convicted of crimes in the 1970s. Many had been radicalized by their imprisonment. They were not interested in working with white antiapartheid activists in organizations such as the UDF. The former BCM members started a new group called the Azanian People's Organization, or AZAPO. (Azania is a name for Africa and comes from ancient Greek mythology.)

Only blacks, mixed race, or Indians could be members of AZAPO. Communism was the guiding ideology of the group. Members called for the violent overthrow of the South African government and the destruction of the entire capitalist system throughout Africa. AZAPO members

AZAPO protests a visit to South Africa by U.S. Senator Edward Kennedy in the 1980s. The group did not support capitalist economies, such as that of the United States.

scorned antiapartheid activists who sought negotiations with Botha.

The ideological clashes between AZAPO and the UDF resulted in more violence. Members of both groups used bottles filled with flaming gasoline, called Molotov cocktails, to destroy homes and murder opposition leaders. Despite their differences, most members of AZAPO and UDF deeply respected Nelson Mandela. They both considered him a saint of the antiapartheid movement.

By 1985 Mandela had been imprisoned for twenty-three years. By the early eighties, activists all over the world had begun calling for his release. As a result, Mandela, who

Prime Minister Pieter W. Botha, shown here at a press conference in the mid-1980s, reached out to Mandela but wasn't yet willing to bring apartheid to an end.

was sixty-seven years old, was one of the world's most famous political prisoners. People inside and outside South Africa believed that Mandela was the only person who could end apartheid and bring peace to the troubled nation. Even Botha came to believe that Mandela could calm the violent masses. He offered to release Mandela if he "unconditionally rejected violence as a political instrument." Mandela responded in a letter, read by his daughter Zindzi at a UDF rally:

I am surprised at the conditions that the government wants to impose on me. I am not a violent man. . . . Let Botha . . . renounce violence. Let him say that he will dismantle apartheid. Let him unban the people's organization, the African National Congress. Let him free all who have been imprisoned, banished or exiled for their opposition to apartheid. Let him guarantee free political activity so that people may decide who will govern them. I cherish my own freedom dearly, but I care even more for your freedom.

Above: Mandela talks with fellow prisoner Walter Sisulu at Robben Island.
Left: Zindzi Mandela reads her father's letter rejecting a conditional release from prison in 1985.

Having failed to draw Mandela to his side, Botha enacted new laws to deal with the crises in the townships. He declared a state of emergency in Sharpeville, the first since 1960, and extended it throughout the nation in 1986. The state of emergency gave police the power to arrest anyone without a warrant and hold them indefinitely without charges. This resulted in thirty thousand detentions. The prisoners' families were not notified, and lawyers were not provided.

■ ■ ■ ECONOMIC SANCTIONS

News coverage of the chaos in South Africa sparked strong antiapartheid sentiments in governing bodies throughout the world. In 1985 and 1986, the U.S. House of Representatives approved several bills to enforce economic sanctions (penalties) against South Africa. The bills prohibited individuals or corporations based in the United States from investing in South Africa or importing various products, including gold, from the country. The bills also banned all air travel between the United States and South Africa. In the resolutions, Congress stated that the U.S. government would keep the pressure on until all South Africans could participate in the political, economic, and social life of the country and all political prisoners were freed.

The sanctions resulted in nearly one hundred U.S. corporations pulling their businesses out of South Africa. This hurt the South African economy. But the most damaging effects were caused by large banks that refused to loan the nation money. This caused inflation and further eroded South African living standards, which created more anger in the townships.

In January 1986, Botha finally gave into the pressure, stunning his supporters when he announced that apartheid was an outdated concept. During a speech before the House of Assembly, the president stated:

We believe that human dignity, life, liberty and property of all must be protected, regardless of color, race, creed or religion. We believe that a democratic system of government, which must accommodate all legitimate political aspirations of all the South African communities, must be negotiated. All South Africans must be placed in a position where they can participate in government through their elected representatives.

Most blacks were not impressed with the speech, since the state of emergency remained. The activities of antiapartheid activists still were severely restricted, and the UDF and ANC still were banned. However, the Botha administration did present ways to loosen apartheid restrictions. The president proposed ending the pass law system; restoring citizenship to people living in the homelands; and allowing blacks to own farms, shops, and businesses.

A BETTER PLACE FOR ALL

Botha suffered a minor stroke on January 20, 1989, and decided to resign in August. He was replaced by Frederik W. de Klerk, the former minister of national education. De Klerk was known as a courteous and pragmatic man. He was a moderate who felt that black citizens needed to be brought into South Africa's political process. Almost immediately, he began secret negotiations with Mandela to start moving South Africa away from apartheid.

On February 2, 1990, de Klerk shocked the nation when he announced the unbanning of the ANC, the PAC, the SACP, and the UDF. De Klerk also informed all freedom fighters that they could

A man holds up a newspaper announcing that the ANC and other political organizations have been unbanned on February 2, 1990.

put down their arms and come to the negotiating table to take part in preparing a new, multiracial constitution. In addition, the president announced that his administration would begin investigating the human rights abuses committed by the police, the BOSS, and other authorities. Upon announcing the transformation of South African society, de Klerk stated: "Our country and all its people have been embroiled [caught] in conflict, tension and violent struggle for decades. It is time for us to break out of the cycle of violence and break through to peace and reconciliation."

In another historic move that made headlines around the world, de Klerk released Mandela from prison on February 11, 1990. The seventy-one-year-old founder of the ANC Youth League had served twenty-seven years in prison for his political activities. Upon his release, millions of joyous South Africans took to the streets to celebrate.

Winnie and Nelson Mandela celebrate his release from prison in February 1990 after twenty-seven years.

Mandela planned to give a speech in Cape Town. But on the way to the event, his motorcade was surrounded by thousands of well-wishers who pounded on the windows and jumped on the roof, the hood, and the trunk. He feared the crowd might kill him with their love. However, he eventually made his way to city hall, where he stood on the balcony and spoke to a sea of people cheering, singing, and waving flags and banners. Mandela stated that he was not a prophet but a humble servant of the people. He thanked them for their tireless work. Finally, the ANC leader made it clear that his release was not part of any kind of deal with de Klerk:

> I wish to report to you that my talks with the government have been aimed at normalizing the political situation in this country. I wish to stress that I myself have at no time entered into negotiations about the future of our country except to insist on a meeting between the ANC and the government.

While black South Africans rejoiced, Mandela spoke of ANC objectives that frightened many whites. In the days that followed, he demanded an immediate release of all political prisoners and the nationalization, or government takeover, of major sectors of the economy, including the gold and diamond industries. Mandela refused to criticize the continuing armed struggle, while calling for international economic sanctions to remain in place until further progress was made.

A NEW NONRACIAL SOUTH AFRICA

Mandela held a historic press conference the next day, packed with reporters from all over the world. Most expected him to be bitter and call for revenge against the government that had held him captive for more than ninety-eight hundred days. Instead, Mandela said:

> I knew people expected me to harbor anger toward whites. But I had none. In prison, my anger toward whites decreased, but

my hatred for the system [of apartheid] grew. I wanted South Africa to see that I loved even my enemies while I hated the system that turned us against one another. . . . Whites are fellow South Africans and we want them to feel safe and know that we appreciate the contributions that they have made toward the development of this country. . . . [We] must do everything we can to persuade our white compatriots that a new nonracial South Africa will be a better place for all.

On his third day of freedom, Mandela climbed aboard a helicopter and flew over Soweto. Even from the air, he could tell that the poverty among the tin shacks and dirt roads was far worse than before he went to prison. Mandela's helicopter landed in the middle of Soweto's eighty-thousand-seat soccer stadium, which was overcrowded with 120,000 cheering admirers. While many expected their hero to promote revolution and call for retribution, Mandela delivered a tough message that centered on the severe problems Africans faced every day. He scolded gangsters who posed as freedom fighters while calling for black-on-black violence in the name of liberty. Mandela begged young people to quit gangs and return to the classroom. He called on the government to build more schools and hire more teachers. Near the end of his thirty-minute speech, Mandela deplored the poverty and suffering endured by Soweto's 2.5 million residents. He reassured the crowd that the ANC would continue to fight as long as apartheid existed.

■ ■ ■ SUSPICION ON ALL SIDES

In March 1990, Mandela was elected deputy president of the ANC. But despite his revered status, the new leader could not unite the splintered antiapartheid movement. Some, especially those in the ANC, supported Mandela's call for peaceful reconciliation. However, groups such as the Pan Africanist Congress rejected the idea of creating a new multiracial government, demanding that the African majority seize power. Another faction, made up of exiled freedom fighters, wanted to continue the armed struggle until the whites offered unconditional surrender.

On February 13, 1990, soon after his release from prison, Nelson Mandela visited Soweto and addressed a rally there. He talked about past injustices and impressed on the people the need to face the future with dignity:

> Today, my return to Soweto fills my heart with joy. At the same time I also return with a deep sense of sadness. Sadness to learn that you are still suffering under an inhuman system. The housing shortage, the schools crisis, unemployment and the crime rate still remain. . . .
>
> As proud as I am to be part of the Soweto community, I have been greatly disturbed by the statistics of crime that I have read in the newspapers. Although I understand the deprivations our people suffer I must make it clear that the level of crime in our township is unhealthy and must be eliminated as a matter of urgency. . . .
>
> The crisis in education that exists in South Africa demands special attention. The education crisis in black schools is a political crisis. It arises out of the fact that our people have no vote and therefore cannot make the government of the day responsive to their needs. Apartheid education is inferior and a crime against humanity. Education is an area that needs the attention of all our people, students, parents, teachers, workers and all other organized sectors of our community. . . .
>
> I call in the strongest possible way for us to act with the dignity and discipline that our just struggle for freedom deserves. Our victories must be celebrated in peace and joy.

Communists insisted on a policy of nationalization that would allow the new government to seize private businesses and corporations. And black revolutionaries living in the townships continued the violence against black officials who worked with the white government. To some observers, it looked as if a civil war might break out in South Africa with the freedom fighters battling one another.

In June 1990, as tensions continued to mount, Mandela led a group of ANC members to Cape Town to negotiate constitutional changes with the de Klerk government. First, the government had to grant immunity (legal protection) to banned and exiled ANC leaders so they could attend the meeting without facing arrest. De Klerk also had to negotiate with his constituency (supporters), some of whom were calling for his resignation and a return to strict apartheid.

Suspicions were high, and talks dragged on for months. Both sides struggled to keep their supporters in line while working out difficult issues with their opponents. Still, many important agreements were hammered out between Mandela and de Klerk. In August the ANC agreed, for the first time since 1960, to suspend its military and sabotage operations. In early October, the National Party agreed to allow nonwhites to join its ranks. And on October 15, the government repealed the Reservation of

F. W. de Klerk and Nelson Mandela shake hands during negotiations between the South African government and the ANC in 1990. The two were awarded the Nobel Peace Prize in 1993 for their work in bringing about the end of apartheid in South Africa.

Separate Amenities Act of 1953, which had implemented the countless petty apartheid laws that remained in place in some areas.

The laws of apartheid continued to fall. The Group Areas Act and the Population Registration Act were repealed in 1990. In February 1991, South African political prisoners were released. In June, the Native Land Acts of 1913 and 1936 and the Group Areas Act of 1950 were dissolved. With this, the government allowed all races equal rights to own property anywhere in the country. Three hundred thousand Africans bought property they had been leasing. The hated pass laws and the Population Registration Act of 1950 were repealed on June 17, 1991.

In September 1991, a thirty-three-page document called the National Peace Accord moved South Africa one step closer to a democratic society. Twenty-seven political organizations and the national and homeland governments signed. The accord outlined formal codes of nonracist conduct for all government officials, including police. It also set up peace committees designed to halt the violence in the townships. Nevertheless, violence continued for months after the National Peace Accord went into effect.

■ ■ ■ A NEW CONSTITUTION

No one believed ending more than four decades of apartheid would be easy. But few were prepared for the increase in political violence. Members of the MK clashed with the PAC and other African organizations in the townships. Gang wars and the necklacing of black officials continued. Problems were intensified by white police and military officers, who wanted apartheid to remain. These groups formed Afrikaner militias. Their members targeted African leaders and used random violence to create distrust and chaos in the townships. Statistics illustrate the problem. In 1989 more than 1,400 people were killed by political violence. In 1991 that number rose to 3,699.

Despite the violence, the U.S. Congress lifted economic sanctions against South Africa in July 1991. European nations followed several months later. The economic progress helped convince most whites that the time had come to end apartheid. A 1992 referendum asked voters "Do you support continuation of the reform process which the State President began on February 2, 1990, and which is aimed at a new constitution through negotiation?" More than 68 percent of South African whites voted yes.

The government body in charge of negotiating an end to apartheid was called the Convention for a Democratic South Africa, or CODESA. In early 1992, de Klerk proposed a plan to manage the transition to democracy by writing a new constitution. Negotiations broke down in July. That month forty-six ANC members, mostly women and children, were gunned down in Boipatong, a township near Vanderbijlpark in Transvaal Province. Although the killers were never identified, many suspected white militias were behind the slaughter. Blacks blamed the government for failing to protect its citizens.

After the massacre, the ANC withdrew from the CODESA negotiations. In the weeks that followed, South Africa was rocked by riots, strikes, demonstrations, civil disobedience, and random killings. The new wave of violence was a turning point, however. It pushed negotiators to settle their differences and create a new government. As de Klerk stated, "The simple truth is that a devastating war will ensue if negotiation does not succeed."

Finally, a new constitution was completed on July 26, 1993. Designed to satisfy all sides in the negotiations, the document called for a federal (central) system of legislators from all regions, equal voting rights regardless of race, and a National Assembly to act as a governing body. The document also set April 26, 1994, as the date for elections.

PRESIDENT MANDELA

It was no surprise that the run-up to the election did not go smoothly. Several political parties, white and nonwhite, struggled to gain power. However, in the first multiracial general election in South African history, more than 22 million people lined up for hours at nine thousand polling places to cast their votes. The election took three days. When the votes were counted, ANC candidates received more than 62 percent of the vote. The NP took about 20 percent of the vote. Eight other political parties also won seats in the National Assembly.

In April 1994, on the eve of South Africa's historic elections, the nation's map was redrawn. The Bantustans once again became an official part of the country. With the addition of new geographic areas, the nation's four provinces were split into nine. Cape Province became: the Western Cape, the Eastern Cape, the Northern Cape, and part of the North West Province. Transvaal Province ceased to exist. It was divided into Gauteng, Limpopo, and Mpumalanga provinces. The former Transvaal also contained most of the North West Province. Other provinces were renamed. Orange Free State became Free State, while Natal was designated KwaZulu-Natal to reflect that it was home to the former KwaZulu Bantustan.

MODERN SOUTH AFRICA

Mandela was unanimously elected president by the National Assembly on May 9, 1994. When he was inaugurated the next day in Pretoria, he was joined by his two deputy presidents, former ANC chairman Thabo Mbeki and former president de Klerk. The historic ceremony was attended by princes, prime ministers, presidents, and other representatives from 140 countries. In his inaugural address, Mandela stressed the need for peace and reconciliation:

> We are both humbled and elevated by the honor and privilege that you, the people of South Africa, have bestowed on us, as the first President of a united, democratic, non-racial and non-sexist government. We understand it still that there is no easy road to freedom. . . . We must therefore act together as a united people, for national reconciliation, for nation building, for the birth of a new world. Let there be justice for all. Let there be peace for all. Let there be work, bread, water and salt for all. Let each know that for each the body, the mind and the soul have been freed to fulfill themselves. Never, never and never again shall it be that this beautiful land will again experience the oppression of one by another and suffer the indignity of being

Nelson Mandela takes the oath of office to become South Africa's first black president on May 10, 1994.

the skunk of the world. Let freedom reign. The sun shall never set on so glorious a human achievement! God bless Africa!

FREEDOM, DEMOCRACY, AND HOPE

Mandela hoped to smooth the transition from apartheid to democracy by forming the Truth and Reconciliation Commission (TRC) to heal the wounds of the nation. Authorized by the "Promotion of National Unity and Reconciliation Act" of 1995, the commission investigated human rights violations committed by the apartheid government, the ANC, and others between 1960 and 1994.

Chaired by Archbishop Tutu, the TRC conducted dozens of public hearings throughout South Africa. More than twenty-one thousand victims and their families provided grisly details about detentions, abductions, beatings, burnings, torture, rape, and murders by government officials. Police, military officers, and other white officials were offered amnesty (pardon) if they truthfully testified and confessed to their political crimes. White South African citizens also testified about crimes committed by the ANC. The TRC finished its work in July 1998. A 3,500-page report on October 28 condemned both sides for committing atrocities.

A witness *(center)* testifies to the TRC on April 15, 1996.

In addition to authorizing the TRC, Mandela made a series of sweeping reforms. Billions of dollars were spent to build schools, clinics, roads, sewers, and electricity. Bringing prosperity to South Africans after decades of warfare, racial violence, and economic inequality was not an easy task. Even as Mandela and a black majority governed the nation in the second half of the 1990s, most of South Africa's economy remained in the hands of the wealthy, educated, white minority.

Mandela chose not to run for a second term in 1999, and he was succeeded by Thabo Mbeki. Under Mbeki's leadership, the number of blacks joining the middle class continued to grow. However, South Africa continued to have one of the highest crime rates in the world. The nation was also suffering from a serious AIDS epidemic. In 2008, when Mbeki completed his last term, the unemployment rate in South Africa was above 48 percent among blacks, one of the highest rates in the world. And about 10 percent of the population was desperately poor, living on less than one dollar a day.

In 2009 Mbeki was replaced by the deputy president, Jacob Zuma. As a former ANC intelligence officer, Zuma created fear among white voters. His campaign theme song, "Um'shini Wam'," in Zulu, or "Bring Me My Machine Gun," caused some to believe Zuma was promoting a new race war. Even before his election, Zuma created controversy. In 2005 he was accused of bribery and offenses relating to political corruption. He also stood trial for rape but was acquitted.

South Africa has undoubtedly faced growing pains since Mandela's election put an end to apartheid. But no one can deny that the historic struggle that began with the Defiance Campaign has changed the country for the better. After fighting for a democratic constitution for decades, the people are free to decide their own fate. The color of a person's skin no longer determines that person's position in society. As Mandela stated at his inauguration, "We have, at last, achieved our political emancipation [freedom]. We pledge ourselves to liberate all our people from the continuing bondage of poverty, deprivation, suffering, gender and other discrimination." While the tasks that lie ahead will not be easy, the new South Africa can look forward with hope to a future of freedom and democracy.

1652: In April the Dutch commander Jan van Riebeeck lands in present-day Cape Town with his wife and son and a crew of eighty-two men and eight women.

1809: The Hottentot Code requires all free blacks to carry passes stating where they live and for whom they work.

1836: Blacks are granted voting rights in the Cape Colony. Afrikaners react by taking the Great Trek to the South African interior.

1866: Erasmus Stephanus Jacobs finds a large diamond on a bank of the Orange River.

1886: Huge gold deposits are found in the hills of the Witwatersrand range, an area called the Rand.

1893: The young lawyer Mohandas Karamchand Gandhi arrives in South Africa, where he forms the Natal Indian Congress (NIC) to fight discrimination.

1899: The British begin the three-year Boer War to capture Transvaal from the Afrikaners.

1910: On May 31, the British parliament approves the Act of Union uniting the four separate colonies to form the Union of South Africa.

1912: The South African Native National Congress is formed. The name is later shortened to the African National Congress, or ANC.

1913: The Native Lands Act sets aside 7.3 percent of South Africa's lands for black people and gives the remaining 92.7 percent to whites.

1918: On July 18, Nelson Mandela is born.

1944: Nelson Mandela, Oliver Tambo, and others form the ANC Youth League.

1948: The National Party wins the South African election and begins passing the laws of apartheid.

1950: On June 26, the ANC Youth League holds its first protest action, the National Day of Protest, aided by the South African Indian Congress, the Communist Party of South Africa, and the African People's Organization.

1952: On June 26, the African National Congress and other antiapartheid groups begin the Defiance Campaign.

1955: On June 25 and 26, the Congress of the People writes the Freedom Charter demanding democracy, equality, and economic fairness in South Africa.

1959: The Promotion of Bantu Self-Government Act creates eight Bantu homelands, or Bantustans.

1960: On March 21, police kill 69 protesters and wound 186 others in the Sharpeville Massacre.

1961: On December 16, Mandela founds the Umkhonto we Sizwe (MK), or Spear of the Nation, to begin an armed struggle against apartheid.

1962: Mandela is convicted of leaving the country illegally and sentenced to five years in jail.

1964: On June 12, Mandela is sentenced to life in prison.

1969: Steve Biko founds the South African Students' Organisation (SASO), the group behind South Africa's Black Consciousness Movement.

1976: On June 16, the Soweto uprising begins.

1983: In August ten thousand delegates of all races form the United Democratic Front (UDF) to oppose apartheid.

1990: On February 11, Nelson Mandela is released from prison after serving twenty-seven years of a life sentence.

1991: Most apartheid-era laws are repealed, and the National Peace Accord is signed.

1994: On May 9, Nelson Mandela becomes South Africa's first black president.

1999: Mandela retires, and Thabo Mbeki is elected president.

2008: Jacob Zuma is elected president of South Africa.

2010: South Africa hosts the FIFA (Fédération Internationale de Football Association) World Cup international soccer tournament—the first time an African nation has been awarded this honor.

Steve Biko

(1946–1977) Biko founded the all-black South African Students' Organisation in 1969, which transformed into the Black Consciousness Movement in the early 1970s. Biko was banned in March 1973, which prevented him from speaking to more than one person at a time during the height of 1970s' apartheid protests. However, he ignored government restrictions and played an important role in organizing the 1976 Soweto Uprising. This activity prompted the government to arrest him and hold him without charges. In 1977, after being tortured and beaten, Biko died of massive head injuries. His funeral was attended by more than fifteen thousand people, including ambassadors and diplomats from the United States and twelve other Western democracies.

Pieter Willem Botha

(1916–2006) Botha was prime minister of South Africa from 1978 to 1984, a period of violent antiapartheid protests and repressive government crackdowns. A longtime leader of the National Party, Botha was a pragmatic conservative who understood that apartheid could not survive. In 1983 he promoted a new South African constitution that granted parliamentary representation to people of mixed race and Indians. Botha also worked to loosen petty apartheid and restrictions on interracial marriage.

Yusuf Mohamed Dadoo

(1909–1983) Dadoo was a South African Communist of Indian heritage. As a member of the South African Indian Congress, Dadoo took a leading role in the Defiance Campaign. Afterward, he was banned but lived underground and secretly worked against apartheid.

Frederik W. de Klerk

(1936–) De Klerk became South Africa's last apartheid president in 1989. During his term, de Klerk worked closely with Nelson Mandela to abolish apartheid and reshape South Africa after more than four decades of segregation. De Klerk won a Nobel Peace Prize in 1993 for his efforts to transform South Africa into a multiracial democracy. After Mandela was elected president of South Africa in 1994, de Klerk served as vice president in the government of national unity.

Mohandas Karamchand Gandhi

(1869–1948) Gandhi was a revered Indian leader who helped his country win independence from Great Britain in 1948. Gandhi first turned to political activism while working as a lawyer in South Africa in 1893. To protest state-enforced segregation, Gandhi developed the philosophy of satyagraha, the non-violence force born of truth and love. In 1906 Gandhi developed a movement of passive resistance against repressive anti-Indian laws. His methods provided inspiration to Nelson Mandela and others during the Defiance Campaign of 1952.

James Barry Munnik Hertzog

(1866–1943) Hertzog was South Africa's minister of native affairs in 1912 when he drafted the Native Lands Act. The law set aside 7.3 percent of the land in the Union of South Africa as reserves for black people, while granting the remaining 92.7 percent of the land to whites. This state-enforced segregation provided a foundation for apartheid and kept Africans crowded into impoverished townships and Bantustans, or homelands, until 1994.

Daniel François Malan

(1874–1959) Malan was a key figure in forming the National Party in 1934. He was elected prime minister in 1948. Malan formed the first all-Afrikaner government since the creation of South Africa in 1910. He put in place a detailed program of apartheid based on the belief that whites were superior to nonwhites. His administration created laws that gave government extraordinary powers to stifle free speech, demonstrations, strikes, and civil disobedience.

Nelson Mandela

(1918–) The revered leader of South Africa's antiapartheid movement, Mandela helped create the African National Congress Youth League in 1944, revitalizing the ANC. In 1952 Mandela was one of the primary forces behind the Defiance Campaign, which led to his banning and arrest. After failing to stop apartheid peacefully, Mandela founded the Umkhonto we Sizwe (MK), or Spear of the Nation. This group waged an armed struggle against apartheid until the 1990s. Mandela was sent to prison for life on June 12, 1964, and remained in jail until February 1990. After his release, he helped end apartheid and was given the 1993 Nobel Peace Prize for his efforts. Mandela was elected the first black president of South Africa in 1994 and retired from politics in 1999.

Cecil Rhodes

(1853–1902) Rhodes was a British-born businessman who made a fortune in the diamond fields of Kimberley in the 1870s. He was a founder of De Beers Consolidated Mines. The company gained almost total control of the diamond industry by the end of the 1880s. Rhodes worked with the government to put a kind of prison system in place at his mines so that he totally controlled the lives of the black miners. As part of a colonial conquest of Africa, Rhodes founded the nation of Rhodesia at the end of the nineteenth century. The country, north of South Africa, was renamed Zimbabwe when it achieved independence in 1980.

Pixley ka Isaka Seme

(1881–1951) A Zulu leader and lawyer, Seme helped found the leading antiapartheid group, the South African Native National Congress (SANNC) in 1912. The name was shortened to the African National Congress, or ANC, in 1923. To publicize the work of the SANNC, Seme started the *Abantu-Batho*, the first South African newspaper published by a black African. Seme was elected president-general of the ANC in 1930. He remained a powerful force in the organization until 1939.

Walter Sisulu

(1912–2003) Sisulu was a friend and mentor to Nelson Mandela. As the secretary-general of the ANC, Sisulu was the driving force behind the group. He was instrumental in organizing the Defiance Campaign as a member of the ANC Joint Planning Council. After being placed under house arrest (forbidden by the courts to leave his house) in 1962, Sisulu went underground. He was arrested and sentenced to life imprisonment in 1964. He was jailed for almost twenty-six years. After his release in October 1989, Sisulu was elected ANC deputy president.

Oliver Tambo

(1917–1993) Tambo was one of the founders of the ANC Youth League in 1944. He also worked as a law partner with Nelson

Mandela. He was named secretary-general of the ANC in 1955. He became deputy president of the organization four years later. After being banned by the government, Tambo moved to London, where he served as acting president of the ANC until 1990. While living in Britain, Tambo worked to end apartheid by promoting economic and political sanctions against South Africa.

Afrikaans: a form of the Dutch language spoken by South Africa's early Dutch settlers

apartheid: the Afrikaans word for "apartness, or separateness," used to describe South Africa's system of racial segregation put in place legally in 1948

Bantu: a term used to describe a family of languages spoken mainly in southern and eastern Africa. During apartheid the term was used by the Nationalist government as a derogatory term for black Africans.

Coloured: the classification given to South Africans of mixed race

Communism: a system of government based on the belief that the wealth and resources of a nation belong equally to all of its citizens

defiance: open or bold refusal to obey laws or rules

homelands: territories set aside for black South Africans under apartheid, also referred to as Bantustans

nationalism: support of national independence

propaganda: ideas or information spread—often by a government—to enforce a desired mind-set and to strengthen the control of one party or system

sanction: an economic or military restriction enacted, usually by several nations at once, to force another nation to stop violating international law

satyagraha: literally, "love and firmness," a philosophy created by Gandhi to describe nonviolent resistance to authority

suppression: a forceful action to put an end to something, destroy it, or prevent it from becoming known

townships: underdeveloped urban living areas built on the edges of South African towns and cities and reserved for nonwhites. These areas typically lacked basic sanitation, electricity, and safe housing.

trekboers: Afrikaner farmers of the 1830s and 1840s who did not live in permanent homes but roamed the countryside grazing their cattle on open lands

United Nations: an international organization formed at the end of World War II in 1945 to help handle global disputes. The United Nations replaced a similar, earlier group known as the League of Nations.

6   Nelson Mandela, *This Struggle Is My Life* (New York: Pathfinder, 1990), 34.

6   Ibid.

7   M. P. Naicker, "The Defiance Campaign Recalled," African National Congress, n.d., http://www.anc.org.za/ancdocs/history/misc/defi-52.html (November 12, 2009).

7   Mary Benson, *The African Patriots* (London: Faber and Faber, 1963), 184.

7   Ibid., 184.

8   J. C. Buthelezi, *Rolihlahla Dalibhunga Nelson Mandela: An Ecological Study* (Victoria, BC: Trafford Books, 2002), 43.

9   Benson, *The African Patriots*, 182.

11 Jan van Riebeeck, *Journal*, part 1 (Cape Town: W. A. Richards & Sons, 1897), 5–6.

16 Henry Lichtenstein, *Travels in Southern Africa in the Years 1803, 1804, 1805, and 1806* (Cape Town: Van Riebeeck Society, 1930), 57.

18 L. E. Neame, *The History of Apartheid* (New York: London House & Maxwell, 1963), 18.

19 Brian Lapping, *Apartheid: A History* (New York: George Braziller, 1987), 19.

20 Ibid., 19.

20 Neame, *The History of Apartheid*, 19.

24 Martin Meredith, *Diamonds, Gold, and War* (New York: Public Affairs, 2007), 13.

26–27 Ibid., 45–46.

28 Perri Giovannucci, *Literature and Development in North Africa: The Modernizing Mission* (New York: Routledge, 2008), 16

31 Jack Simons and Ray Simons, "Diamond Diggers and the New Elite," African National Congress, n.d., http:www.anc.org.za/books/ccsa02.html (November 12, 2009).

31 Lapping, *Apartheid: A History*, 26.

33 Mohandas Gandhi, "Gandhi Explains Satyagraha," South African History, n.d., http://www.sahistory.org.za/pages/library-resources/online%20books/bhana/part01-E-44.htm (November 12, 2009).

38 Kuruvila Pandikattu, ed., *Gandhi: The Meaning of Mahatma for the Millennium* (Washington, DC: Council for Research in Values and Philosophy, 2001), 45.

43 Benson, *The African Patriots*, 28.

44 Ibid., 31.

45 Lapping, *Apartheid: A History*, 55.

45 Heidi Holland, *The Struggle: A History of the African National Congress* (New York: George Braziller, 1989), 42.

45 Ibid., 41.

46 Solomon T. Plaatje, *Native Life in South Africa: Before and Since the European War and the Boer Rebellion* (Athens: Ohio University Press, 1991), 86.

46 Peter Walshe, *Rise of African Nationalism in South Africa* (Berkeley: University of California Press, 1982), 46.

46 Neame, *The History of Apartheid*, 40.

47 Nigel Worden, *The Making of Modern South Africa: Conquest, Segregation, and Apartheid* (Malden, MA: Blackwell Publishing, 2004), 60.

47 Neame, *The History of Apartheid*, 46.

51 Ibid., 50.
52 Naicker, "The Defiance Campaign Recalled."
53–54 Nelson Mandela, *Long Walk to Freedom* (Boston: Little, Brown and Company, 1994), 20–21.
55 Neame, *The History of Apartheid*, 52.
55 Robert A. Hill, ed., *The Marcus Garvey and Universal Negro Improvement Association Papers*, vol. 1 (Berkeley: University of California Press, 1983), lxxviii–lxxxix.
56 Marcus Garvey, "Africa for Africans," Marcus Garvey–the Official Site, January 8, 2004, http://www.marcusgarvey.com/wmview.php?ArtID=48 (November 12, 2009).
56 Morgan Norval, *Inside the ANC* (Washington, DC: Selous Foundation Press, 1990), 33.
58 Chris McGreal, "Brothers in Arms—Israel's Secret Pact with Pretoria," Guardian (London), February 7, 2006, http://www.guardian.co.uk/world/2006/feb/07/southafrica.israel (February 7, 2006).
60 Mandela, *Long Walk to Freedom*, 84.
61 Ibid., 83.
61 Ibid., 87.
62 Ibid., 84.
64 Ibid., 106.
66 G. H. L. Le May, *The Afrikaners: An Historical Interpretation* (Cambridge, MA: Blackwell Publishers, 1995), 209.
67 John Lodge, *Mandela: A Critical Life* (Oxford: Oxford University Press, 2006), 45.
68 African National Congress, "National Day of Protest 1950," ANC, n.d., http://www.anc.org.za/ancdocs/pr/1950s/pr500521.html (November 12, 2009).
70 Naicker, "The Defiance Campaign Recalled."
71 Lodge, *Mandela: A Critical Life*, 51.
71 Mandela, *Long Walk to Freedom*, 104.
72 Ahmad M. Kathrada, *Memoirs* (Cape Town: Zebra Press, 2004), 100.
72 Ibid., 100.
73 Mandela, *Long Walk to Freedom*, 111.
75 Neame, *The History of Apartheid*, 101.
75 Ibid.
75 Holland, *The Struggle*, 78.
77–78 Kathrada, *Memoirs*, 102.
78 Mandela, *Long Walk to Freedom*, 115.
81 Holland, *The Struggle*, 82.
82–83 SAHO, "The 1952 Defiance Campaign," South Africa History Online, n.d., http://www.sahistory.org.za/pages/governance-projects/defiance-campaign/07_defiance-campaign.htm (November 12, 2009).
83 Holland, *The Struggle*, 83.
84 SAHO, "The 1952 Defiance Campaign."
85 Mandela, *Long Walk to Freedom*, 120–121.
86 Lapping, *Apartheid: A History*, 121.
88 Neame, *The History of Apartheid*, 131–132.
89 Frank Welsh, *South Africa: A Narrative History* (New York: Kodansha International, 1999), 444.

90 Naicker, "The Defiance Campaign Recalled."

91–92 Lapping, *Apartheid: A History*, 109.

92 Holland, *The Struggle*, 91.

94 Congress of the People, "The Freedom Charter, 1955," Gandhi-Luthuli Documentation Centre, n.d., http://scnc.ukzn.ac.za/doc/HIST/freedomchart/freedomch.html (February 15, 2009).

94 Ibid.

95 Ibid.

98 Lapping, *Apartheid: A History*, 130.

99 South African Democracy Education Trust, *The Road to Democracy in South Africa*, vol. 1, 1960–1970 (Cape Town: Zebra Press, 2004), 39.

101 James Barber, *South Africa in the Twentieth Century* (Malden, MA: Blackwell Publishers, 1999), 165.

101 Ibid., 166.

102 African National Congress, "Umrabulo,"ANC, December 2001, http://www.anc.org.za/show.php?doc=ancdocs/pubs/umrabulo/13/umrabulo13.html#editoria (November 12, 2009).

105 Nelson Mandela, "I Am Prepared to Die," ANC, n.d., http://www.anc.org.za/ancdocs/history/rivonia.html (November 12, 2009).

106 Lapping, *Apartheid: A History*, 155.

107 Ibid., 156.

108 Steve Biko, "Black Consciousness and the Quest for a True Humanity," South African History Online, n.d., http://www.sahistory.org.za/pages/library-resources/articles_papers/1990_biko_humanity_quest.html (November 19, 2009).

109 Lapping, *Apartheid: A History*, 158.

114 "The End of Apartheid and the Birth of Democracy," Michigan State University. n.d., http://overcomingapartheid.msu.edu/unit.php?id=14 (March 13, 2010).

115 Barber, *South Africa in the Twentieth Century*, 225.

115 Ibid.

120–121 Desmond Tutu, "Nobel Lecture," Nobelprize.org, n.d., http://nobelprize.org/nobel_prizes/peace/laureates/1984/tutu-lecture.html (November 12, 2009).

121 Eugene de Kock, *A Long Night's Damage: Working for the Apartheid State* (Saxonwold, South Africa: Contra Press, 1988), 100.

123 Sanderson Beck, "Mandela and Freeing South Africa," *World Peace Efforts since Ganghi*, 2005, http://www.san.beck.org/GPJ34-Mandela.html (November 12, 2009).

123 David H. Anthony, "Luta Continua," UCSD Library Exhibits, 2002, http://library.ucsc.edu/content/a-luta-continua (March 16, 2010).

125–126 Michael Parks, "Botha Outlines Apartheid Reforms; Blacks Unmoved," *Los Angeles Times*, 2009, http://articles.latimes.com/1986-02-01/

news/mn-2917_1_political
-reform (February 12, 2009).

126 Willem de Klerk, *F. W. de
Klerk: The Man in His Times*
Jeppestown, South Africa:
Jonathan Ball, 1991), 36.

128 Mandela, *Long Walk to Freedom*,
493.

128 –129 Ibid.

130 Nelson Mandela, "Nelson
Mandela's Address to Rally
in Soweto," African National
Congress, n.d., http://www
.anc.org.za/ancdocs/history/
mandela/sp900213.html
(November 12, 2009).

132–133 Christopher S. Wren,
"Turnout Heavy as South
Africans Vote on Change," *New
York Times*, n.d., http://www

.nytimes.com/1992/03/18/
world/turnout-heavy-as
-south-africans-vote-on
-change.html?pagewanted=all
(September 17, 2009).

133 Barber, *South Africa in the
Twentieth Century*, 295.

135–136 Nelson Mandela, "Statement
of the President of the African
National Congress Nelson
Rolihlahla Mandela at His
Inauguration as President
of the Democratic Republic
of South Africa Union
Buildings," African National
Congress, n.d., http://www
.anc.org.za/ancdocs/history/
mandela/1994/inaugpta.html
(November 12, 2009).

137 Ibid.

SELECTED BIBLIOGRAPHY

African National Congress. "National Day of Protest 1950." ANC, N.d. http://www.anc.org.za/ancdocs/pr/1950s/pr500521.html (November 12, 2009).

———. "Umrabulo." ANC. December 2001. http://www.anc.org.za/show.php?doc=ancdocs/pubs/umrabulo/13/umrabulo13.html#editoria (November 12, 2009).

Anthony, David H. "Luta Continua." UCSD Library Exhibits. 2002. http://library.ucsc.edu/content/a-luta-continua (March 16, 2010).

Barber, James. *South Africa in the Twentieth Century*. Malden, MA: Blackwell Publishers, 1999.

Beck, Sanderson. "Mandela and Freeing South Africa." *World Peace Efforts since Gandhi*. 2005. http://www.san.beck.org/GPJ34-Mandela.html (November 19, 2009).

Benson, Mary. *The African Patriots*. London: Faber and Faber, 1963.

Biko, Steve. "Black Consciousness and the Quest for a True Humanity." South African History Online. N.d. http://www.sahistory.org.za/pages/library-resources/articles_papers/1990_biko_humanity_quest.html (November 19, 2009).

Congress of the People. "The Freedom Charter, 1955." Gandhi-Luthuli Documentation Centre. N.d. http://scnc.ukzn.ac.za/doc/HIST/freedomchart/freedomch.html (February 15, 2009).

De Klerk, Willem. *F. W. de Klerk: The Man in His Times*. Jeppestown, South Africa: Jonathan Ball, 1991.

De Kock, Eugene. *A Long Night's Damage: Working for the Apartheid State*. Saxonwold, South Africa: Contra Press, 1988.

Gandhi, Mohandas. "Gandhi Explains Satyagraha." South African History. N.d. http://www.sahistory.org.za/pages/library-resources/online%20books/bhana/part01-E-44.htm (November 12, 2009).

Garvey, Marcus. "Africa for Africans." Marcus Garvey—the Official Site. January 8, 2004. http://www.marcusgarvey.com/wmview.php?ArtID=48 (November 12, 2009).

Hill, Robert A., ed. *The Marcus Garvey and Universal Negro Improvement Association Papers*. Vol. 1. Berkeley: University of California Press, 1983.

Holland, Heidi. *The Struggle: A History of the African National Congress*. New York: George Braziller, 1989.

Jeter, John. "For South Africa's Poor,. . . . A New Power Struggle." *Washington Post*, August 8, 2006. http://www.washingtonpost.com/wp-dyn/content/article/2006/08/08/AR2006080800826.html (November 12, 2009).

Kathrada, Ahmad M. *Memoirs*. Cape Town: Zebra Press, 2004.

Lapping, Brian. *Apartheid: A History*. New York: George Braziller, 1987.

Le May, G. H. L. *The Afrikaners: An Historical Interpretation*. Cambridge, MA: Blackwell Publishers, 1995.

Lichtenstein, Henry. *Travels in Southern Africa in the Years 1803, 1804, 1805, and 1806*. Cape Town: Van Riebeeck Society, 1930.

Lodge, John. *Mandela: A Critical Life*. Oxford: Oxford University Press, 2006.

Mandela, Nelson. "I Am Prepared to Die." ANC. N.d. http://www.anc.org.za/ancdocs/history/rivonia.html (November 12, 2009).

———. *Long Walk to Freedom*. Boston: Little, Brown and Company, 1994.

———. "Nelson Mandela's Address to Rally in Soweto." ANC, N.d. http://www.anc.org.za/ancdocs/history/mandela/sp900213.html (November 12, 2009).

———. "Statement of the President of the African National Congress Nelson Rolihlahla Mandela at His Inauguration as President of the Democratic Republic of South Africa Union Buildings." ANC. N.d. http://www.anc.org.za/ancdocs/history/mandela/1994/inaugpta.html (November 12, 2009).

———. *This Struggle Is My Life*. New York: Pathfinder, 1990.

McGreal, Chris. "Brothers in Arms—Israel's Secret Pact with Pretoria." *Guardian* (London). February 7, 2006. http://www.guardian.co.uk/world/2006/feb/07/southafrica.israel (March 15, 2010).

Meredith, Martin. *Diamonds, Gold, and War*. New York: Public Affairs, 2007.

Naicker, M. P. "The Defiance Campaign Recalled." African National Congress. N.d. http://www.anc.org.za/ancdocs/history/misc/defi-52.html (November 12, 2009).

Neame, L. E. *The History of Apartheid*. New York: London House & Maxwell, 1963.

Norval, Morgan. *Inside the ANC*. Washington, DC: Selous Foundation Press, 1990.

Pandikattu, Kuruvila, ed. *Gandhi: The Meaning of Mahatma for the Millennium*. Washington, DC: Council for Research in Values and Philosophy, 2001.

Parks, Michael. "Botha Outlines Apartheid Reforms; Blacks Unmoved." *Los Angeles Times*, N.d. http://articles.latimes.com/1986-02-01/news/mn-2917_1_political-reform (November 12, 2009).

Plaatje, Solomon T. *Native Life in South Africa: Before and Since the European War and the Boer Rebellion*. Athens: Ohio University Press, 1991.

Simons, Jack, and Ray Simons. "Diamond Diggers and the New Elite." African National Congress. N.d. http://www.anc.org.za/books/ccsa02.html (November 12, 2009).

South African Democracy Education Trust. *The Road to Democracy in South Africa.* Vol. 1, 1960–1970. Cape Town: Zebra Press, 2004.

Tutu, Desmond. "Nobel Lecture." Nobelprize.org. N.d. http://nobelprize.org/nobel _prizes/peace/laureates/1984/tutu-lecture.html (November 12, 2009).

Van Riebeeck, Jan. *Journal.* Part 1. Cape Town: W. A. Richards & Sons, 1897.

Walshe, Peter. *Rise of African Nationalism in South Africa.* Berkeley: University of California Press, 1982.

Welsh, Frank. *South Africa: A Narrative History.* New York: Kodansha International, 1999.

Worden, Nigel. *The Making of Modern South Africa: Conquest, Segregation, and Apartheid.* Malden, MA: Blackwell Publishing, 2004.

Wren, Christopher S. "Turnout Heavy as South Africans Vote on Change." *New York Times.* N.d. http://www.nytimes.com/1992/03/18/world/turnout-heavy-as-south-africans-vote-on-change.html?pagewanted=all (September 17, 2009).

Books

Cruden, Alex. *The End of Apartheid*. Detroit: Greenhaven Press, 2009. This book discusses apartheid and how it came to an end with the election of Nelson Mandela as South Africa's first black president.

Finlayson, Reggie. *Nelson Mandela*. Minneapolis: Lerner Publications Company, 2006. This biography covers Mandela's childhood in Xhosa, his training as a lawyer, and his rise through the ranks of the African National Congress.

Gleimius, Nita, Emma Mthimunye, and Evelina Subanyoni. *The Zulu of Africa*. Minneapolis: Lerner Publications Company, 2003. This book reveals Zulu history and culture and how the Zulu have preserved their ancient traditions.

Hamilton, Janice. *South Africa in Pictures*. Minneapolis: Twenty-First Century Books, 2004. This title in the Visual Geography series enhances readers' knowledge of South Africa's geography, people, history, government, economy, and cultural life.

Keller, Bill. *Tree Shaker: The Story of Nelson Mandela*. Boston: Kingfisher, 2008. *New York Times* reporter Keller draws on his years as the Johannesburg bureau chief in this profile that includes the history of white colonization, the fight against apartheid, and Mandela's years as a prisoner on Robben Island.

Mace, Virginia. *South Africa*. Washington, DC: National Geographic, 2008. This is a study of the southernmost African nation, where 47 million people speak eleven official languages. The book covers white settlement, apartheid, and Nelson Mandela's rise to power.

Naidoo, Beverly. *Out of Bounds: Seven Stories of Conflict and Hope*. New York: HarperCollins, 2008. These short personal stories, set in different decades in South Africa, from the 1950s onward, personalize the political oppression of apartheid and struggle for freedom from the viewpoint of a child.

Parker, Linda. *The San of Africa*. Minneapolis: Lerner Publications Company, 2002. This title tells the history of the San and their struggle to keep alive their rich culture within the modern world.

Weltig, Matthew Scott. *The Aftermath of the Anglo-Zulu War*. Minneapolis: Twenty-First Century Books, 2009. This is the painful story of the devastation and ruin brought to Zululand by the British government and Boer settlers in the nineteenth century.

Websites

African National Congress

http://www.anc.org.za

The official website of the African National Congress contains historical documents, articles about current events, and back issues of important ANC publications such as *Mayibuye* and *ANC Today*. The site also follows the latest election news in South Africa and provides links to the ANC Youth League and Women's League websites.

South Africa History Online

http://www.sahistory.org.za

This website was established in 2000 to provide a comprehensive history of South Africa. Its goal is to counter the biased manner in which the country's history and cultural heritage were represented in educational and cultural institutions under apartheid. The site provides a people's history meant to portray a nonracial, nonsexist, and democratic society.

South Africa Today

http://www.southafrica.info/about/satoday.htm

This website follows the latest news in South Africa including politics, travel, sports, and entertainment. Hundreds of beautiful photographs display the distinctive art, architecture, people, parks, wildlife, and history of South Africa.

South African Communist Party

http://www.sacp.org.za

This site is maintained by an organization that fought alongside the ANC to end apartheid. Articles include historical documents, biographies of antiapartheid leaders, and the latest news. The site also allows users to download the SACP magazine *Umsebenzi*.

South African Music

http://www.southafrica.info/about/arts/music.htm

The joyous music that provided the sound track to the antiapartheid movement is featured on this website. Linked articles include the history of South African resistance music, biographies of popular artists, and discussions of the country's unique musical styles.

vgsbooks.com

http://www.vgsbooks.com/

Visit vgsbooks.com, the home page of the Visual Geography Series®. You can get linked to all sorts of useful online information about countries around the world, including geographical, historical, demographic, cultural, and economic websites. The vgsbooks.com site is a great resource for late-breaking news about South Africa.

reserves, 19, 41, 45, 64, 98–99, 106–107
resettlement operations, 106–107
Resha, Robert, 92, 93, 97
Retief, Piet, 20, 21, 22
Rhodes, Cecil, 29, 143–144
riots and violence: Defiance Campaign
    and, 81–83, 84, 85; end of apartheid
    and, 118–121, 132–133; Sharpeville
    and, 99, 100, 101, 118–119, 139;
    townships and, 111, 118–121
Rumpff, F. L. H., 80, 85–86

sanctions, 113, 125–126, 132
San people, 11, 12
segregation, 32–33, 50, 74, 86–87, 107.
    See also apartheid laws
Seme, Pixley ka Isaka, 43, 144
"separate but equal," 86–87
Sharpeville massacre, 99, 100, 101, 139
Sharpeville riots, 118–119
Sisulu, Walter, 144; African National
    Congress (ANC) and, 60, 66; arrests
    and trials, 79, 96, 104–105; Defiance
    Campaign and, 77–78; Freedom
    Charter and, 95
Sita, Nana, 5, 77
slavery, 13, 17, 18, 19
Smuts, Jan, 37–38, 46, 48–49
South African Indian Congress (SAIC),
    68, 72–73, 93
South African Native National Congress
    (SANNC), 42–45, 46–47, 138. *See also*
    African National Congress (ANC)
South African Republic and Boer War,
    34–35
South African Student's Organization
    (SASO), 108, 109
Soweto Township, 110–111, 129, 130, 140

strikes, 47–49, 74. *See also* labor unions
Strydom, Johannes, 88, 89
Suppression of Communism Act (1950),
    5, 65–66, 72–73, 96

Tambo, Oliver, 60, 66, 96, 101, 144–145

taxation, 54
theft, diamonds and, 25, 29–31
Tomlinson Commission, 64
townships, 69, 118–121, 132–133
Transvaal, 37–38, 39
trekboers, 14–17
tribal colleges, 107
Truth and Reconciliation Commission
    (TRC), 136–137
Tutu, Desmond, 117, 120–121, 136

Umkhonto we Sizwe (MK), 101–103,
    106, 113, 139
United Democratic Front (UDF), 117,
    123, 140
United Nations, 101, 112, 113
United States, 111–112, 125
Urban Areas Act, 92

van Riebeeck, Jan, 9–11, 138
Verwoerd, Hendrik Frensch, 82, 91–92,
    98–99, 105–106
violent resistance to apartheid, 101–102,
    106, 113, 122–123, 129, 131. *See also*
    riots and violence
Voortrekkers, 20–21, 22, 23
Vorster, John, 105, 106, 112
voting rights, 19–20, 39–40, 54, 88,
    117, 138

warfare with native Africans, 14, 17,
    21, 22
white Africans and Defiance Campaign,
    83
white supremacy, 88, 89
Wiehahn Commission, 115–116
World War I, 45
World War II, 58, 62

Xhosa people, 16–18, 53

Year of Africa, 101, 102

Zulu people, 20–21, 22
Zuma, Jacob, 137, 140

PHOTO ACKNOWLEDGMENTS

The images in this book are used with the permission of: The Granger Collection, New York, pp. 5, 19, 21, 43; © imagebroker/Alamy, p. 9; © Ariadne Van Zandbergen/ Photolibrary/Getty Images, p. 10; © Print Collector/HIP/The Image Works, p. 15; © INTERFOTO/Alamy, p. 20; The Art Archive/National Archives, Pretoria, p. 22; Courtesy of De Beers, p. 24; © Gray Marrets/Hulton Archive/Getty Images, p. 26; © Hulton Archive/Getty Images, pp. 29, 36 (top); Library of Congress, pp. 30 (LC-USZ62-93985), 42 (LC-DIG-ggbain-32959), 56 (right, LC-USZ61-1854); © Keystone/Hulton Archive/Getty Images, pp. 32, 100 (bottom); © Laura Westlund/ Independent Picture Service, pp. 34, 134; © Paul Popper/Popperfoto/Getty Images, pp. 36 (bottom), 83; © Dinodia Images/Alamy, pp. 38–39; © Photo12/The Image Works, p. 40; © Time & Life Pictures/Getty Images, p. 41; © UWC-Robben Island Museum Mayibuye Archives, pp. 44, 59, 62, 95, 124 (top); © Bettmann/ CORBIS, pp. 48, 50, 56 (left), 65, 69, 79, 116; © BaileysHistory/Africanpictures/ The Image Works, pp. 60, 91, 93 (both), 94, 96, 103, 104; © Nat Farbman/Time & Life Pictures/Getty Images, p. 72; © AFP/Getty Images, pp. 74–75, 112; © Jurgen Schadeberg/Hulton Archive/Getty Images, p. 80; © Margaret Bourke-White/Time & Life Pictures/Getty Images, p. 87; © Dr. Gilbert H. Grosvenor/National Geographic Society/CORBIS, p. 89; AP Photo, pp. 97, 110; AP Photo/Cape Argus, p. 100 (top); © Mark Peters/Getty Images, p. 107; AP Photo/Argus, p. 118; AP Photo/Helmuth Lohmann, p. 121; © Gideon Mendel/CORBIS, p. 122; © Selwyn Tait/Time & Life Pictures/Getty Images, p. 123; AP Photo/Peters, p. 124 (bottom); © Rashid Lombard/ AFP/Getty Images, p. 126; © Allan Tannenbaum/Time & Life Pictures/Getty Images, p. 127; © Louise Gubb/CORBIS SABA, p. 131; AP Photo/David Brauchli, p. 135; AP Photo/Pool-Mike Hutchings, p. 136.

Front cover: © Popperfoto/Getty Images.

ABOUT THE AUTHOR

Stuart A. Kallen has written more than 250 nonfiction books for children and young adults over the past twenty years. His books have covered countless aspects of human history, culture, and science from the building of the pyramids to the music of the twenty-first century. Some of his recent titles include *The Sandinista Revolution*, *Postmodern Art*, and *Harlem Renaissance*. Kallen, who lives in San Diego, California, is also a singer-songwriter and guitarist.